John Buckingham Pope

Railway Rates and Radical Rule

Being a Series of Practical Questions Vitally Affecting the Interests of Traders and Agriculturists throughout the Country, and Suggested to them for Consideration, as Electors

John Buckingham Pope

Railway Rates and Radical Rule

Being a Series of Practical Questions Vitally Affecting the Interests of Traders and Agriculturists throughout the Country, and Suggested to them for Consideration, as Electors

ISBN/EAN: 9783744755795

Printed in Europe, USA, Canada, Australia, Japan

Cover: Foto ©Suzi / pixelio.de

More available books at **www.hansebooks.com**

RAILWAY RATES

AND

RADICAL RULE

BEING

A SERIES OF PRACTICAL QUESTIONS VITALLY AFFECTING
THE INTERESTS OF TRADERS AND AGRICULTURISTS
THROUGHOUT THE COUNTRY, AND SUGGESTED
TO THEM FOR CONSIDERATION, AS
ELECTORS

BY

J. BUCKINGHAM POPE

BARRISTER-AT-LAW

LONDON
KEGAN PAUL, TRENCH & CO., 1, PATERNOSTER SQUARE
1884

CONTENTS.

	PAGE
INTRODUCTORY CHAPTER	1
UNDUE PREFERENCE	11
SHORT DISTANCE CLAUSES	27
SELECT COMMITTEE ON RAILWAY RATES AND FARES, 1881	38
EXTRACTS FROM THE EVIDENCE OF THE TRADING PUBLIC BEFORE SELECT COMMITTEE	53
EXTRACTS FROM RAILWAY EVIDENCE BEFORE SELECT COMMITTEE	129
STATEMENT OF SIR THOMAS FARRER, BART. ...	184
THE THOUGHTFUL LIBERAL	205
LAND	223
IRISH LAND ACTS	234
CLASS LEGISLATION ...	253
FREE TRADE	270
RAILWAY DIRECTORS IN PARLIAMENT	280
RAILWAY COMMISSIONERS' COURT ...	290
TRADERS' "LOCUS STANDI" BEFORE PARLIAMENTARY COMMITTEES	301
COMPETING RAILWAY BILLS IN PARLIAMENT	305
PROPOSED SHIPPING LEGISLATION ...	324
THE EDUCATION ACT OF 1870	335
MR. CHAMBERLAIN'S PROPOSED RAILWAY LEGISLATION	350
CONCLUDING REMARKS	361

RAILWAY RATES AND RADICAL RULE.

INTRODUCTORY CHAPTER.

THE ensuing pages have been written for the purpose of bringing prominently before the public the effects of Radical legislation on the trade, commerce, and taxation of this country, and at the same time of showing, in as practical and concise a manner as possible, that those effects are equalled if not surpassed, in their injurious influence, by the extraordinary absence of legislation for the due protection of the public from the system of Railway government which now rules almost despotically over the trade of this kingdom.

I use the term "government" advisedly, for although it may not have occurred to many of my readers that the people of this country are ruled by any laws save those passed by Parliament, still the fact nevertheless remains, that since our highways were for trade purposes superseded and rendered practically worthless, a great power, created by Parliament, has arisen in our midst, which makes laws and regulations of its own, and imposes taxes on our industries and commercial enterprises (artificially fostering some and heavily taxing others), and performs generally the part of an irresponsible government.

Not only the principles of Acts of Parliament passed for the protection of the public, but even their expressed terms in detail, are openly transgressed.

When Parliament gave authority to Railway Companies to forcibly enter into and break up land in every district in England, it did so in the interests and for the good of the people of England; but the railway legislators have put quite another complexion on the matter, as they have ordained that Englishmen shall not enjoy the same rights over their own railways as foreigners. The foreigner's privilege consists in the right to use the railways for traffic at from twenty to fifty per cent. less than Englishmen; and this is why the Americans and others can undersell the British farmer in his own markets. It is unnecessary, however, here to anticipate facts which will be fully explained in the subsequent chapters. Enough to say that a distinct *imperium in imperio* has been set up amongst us, and that whilst one legislature is spending its days and nights in endless discussions on abstract principles, moral convictions, doctrinaire notions, and the dreams of the faddist, and in banishing all opposing economic influences to the regions of Jupiter and Saturn, our railway legislators are governing the country with a rod of iron, quite contented to see the people " pleased with the rattle and tickled with the toy " of the other Parliament.

Freedom of access to the markets of this country, and also to those of the world generally, are as important to its trade and agriculture as the breath is to the body. That freedom it does not possess; and yet the great reforming party now in power look on with folded hands and apparent indifference. " Earnest and thoughtful Liberals," who are ready at a moment's notice to call in question anything under the sun—to alter or pull down, if possible, any institution on the face of the earth, especially if it has done good service and existed for a long time— have for once in their lives nothing to say. Some of them, on the other hand, directly countenance this railway legislation; whilst others even go so far as to take part in it, by consenting to occupy a seat at the Board when invited so to do by the railway authorities. Need I add that it often occurs that after an individual has added the mystic letters M.P. to his name he *is* invited, and that singularly enough the Railway Companies from that moment see in him the very man they have been looking for to aid them in their business deliberations, and which they have previously been unable to find? In this way it becomes demonstrated that there exists a considerable amount of latent Conservatism, even in Radicals; for when railway questions arise in Parliament, the most pronounced specimen invariably votes "solid" with his brother directors.

But it is only in matters connected with £ s. d., in which he and his friends and relations are more or less interested, that he loses his individuality, which, however, again asserts itself with renewed vigour when dealing with the property of others. It is notorious that, when not personally affected, the modern Radical is in the habit of making very singular discoveries with respect to property, especially in relation to land. He has found out that land belongs to the people, and that, as the people's representative, he has a right to try experiments on what belongs through the people to himself. Grinding and tyrannical landlords are, according to him, the cause of the decadence of British agriculture, and he does not scruple to hint more or less broadly that the two or three per cent. interest on money invested, received by them in the way of rent, may properly, either in whole or in part, be taken from them—not perhaps at one blow, but by a series of confiscatory measures all tending to that object. So busy has he been in posing as the farmers' friend and in airing the endless variety of theories in justification of attacks upon landlords, that he has apparently allowed the very remarkable evidence given before the Select Committee on Railway Rates and Fares to pass unnoticed. This evidence, as my readers will shortly see, points distinctly to the fact that in his railway capacity (either as director or shareholder) the Radical is himself robbing not only the farmer, but the trader. Moreover, the robbery is no sentimental or constructive one, like the receipt of rent, but the simple and ordinary device of taking money which belongs to another. The *modus operandi* consists in charging people for the carriage of goods or produce, in many cases, some two or three hundred per cent. more than the law allows.

We have now had experience of Radical rule for some years; and whilst our trade keeps unremunerative, our taxes grow heavier. The legislature, one of whose chief duties it is to keep a watchful eye over our commerce, and especially over the effects of those private Acts which exercise so direct an influence over it, have absolutely neglected their duties. They knew that the powers of railways for taxing British trade and agriculture had been given almost in the dark on the *ex parte* statement of the Railway Companies. They knew that, these powers having once been given, there was no Court of Revision for the public, however great the injustice or however vast the mistakes. The evidence given before the Select Committee of 1881–2 abundantly showed that mistakes had been made and injustice worked to such an extent as positively to cripple English trade; yet the session of 1883 passed, and the Government made no sign. All the time that could be spared from Irish affairs

—that chaos of their own making—they devoted to attempts to formulate into Acts of Parliament the fads and crochets of their own advanced followers. They certainly passed a Bankruptcy Bill, an Act of grim significance at the present time, evidently determined to prepare for the worst. An Act, however, for freeing our highways and so to a large extent preventing the bankruptcy which is threatening us, would, in the opinion of most people, have been more to the point. No one, who knows anything of these subjects, and who will take the trouble to read the Parliamentary debates of the past session, but will be strongly reminded by them of the "fiddling" which we are told took place whilst "Rome was burning."

The ensuing chapters will be directed not so much to the general review of Radical policy, as to an examination of the monetary effects produced on the country by measures which have lately become law. Acts which have been passed at different times and discussed solely on their individual merits may appear to possess small financial importance, yet when regarded collectively they assume very different proportions; and it is their cumulative effects to which I wish to draw the attention of my readers, reminding them at the same time of the interminable number of similar measures which are even now simmering in "thoughtful" minds, and which will ere long develop into "burning questions."

With regard to railways, without mystifying my readers with long tables, classification of rates, masses of figures, and technical terms which only tend to confuse the uninitiated, and which confusion has proved the sheet anchor of the Railway Companies on many trying occasions, I shall endeavour to point out as broadly as possible some of the notorious evils appertaining to the present system, and will only refer to details in order to prove the truth of my assertions.

I know well there is no difficulty in this portion of the task. Times without number witnesses have dilated on these glaring evils before Parliamentary Committees. The real difficulty always arises when some skilled railway cross-examiner (with which individual the committees are generally well supplied) asks a witness, "What alterations do you propose?" Then, if the latter is entrapped into a hurried or thoughtless answer, he is immediately tripped up and made to look foolish, and the lay members of the committee probably become as bewildered as the witness. The railway directors have, then, little difficulty in bringing in a verdict of "Not Guilty," coupled probably with some weak suggestions, as a sop to those members who, although not agreeing with the decision, are at a loss to know what to propose.

It is, in my opinion, no use to bring forward a grievance unless practical remedies can be shown and remedies consistent with the acts the Railway Companies now possess; for, however wrong Parliament may have been in granting such Acts, and however forgetful of the interests of the public, the evil is done, and anything of a confiscating nature is not to be thought of for a moment. This country requires no legislation on the lines of the Irish Land Act, and had far better bear its burdens, however grievous, than ask for the confiscation of rights which, being once legally granted, cannot be taken away without shaking the foundations of the whole fabric on which society rests. I therefore propose, having mentioned the evils, to point out at the end of each chapter the remedies which, in my humble judgment, may be applied without in any way trespassing on the rights of the Railway Companies. In other words, I propose to review the rights of the public, which Parliament has so long allowed to be trampled on, and to which the present Government have, up to this time, manifested such sublime indifference. If traders and agriculturists are to be rescued from the present Slough of Despond, it is necessary that the legislators of this country should be clearly made to understand that the first duty of a Government in home policy is to protect them from State-made monopolies, and that such measures as the Extension of the Suffrage, Municipal Corporation, Local Option, Corrupt Practices Acts, etc., etc., although surrounded by the glamour of sentiment, are not the kind of things on which the traders, farmers, and working men of England can live. These people are infinitely more interested in trying to solve the problem of how to support their wives and families than they are in the ethereal food with which the Government has so long surfeited them. The English people have been asked to live on sentiment quite long enough; and if they are to keep body and soul together, it is high time they had a change of diet.

UNDUE PREFERENCE.

THE chief issue between the public and the Railway Companies is this, "Shall the latter be compelled to carry at the same rate of payment for one individual as for another?" and upon the answer the future prosperity of England's commerce and agriculture depends? In so many words it means, are Railway Companies to be put on the same footing as other trading companies—doing a certain amount of work for a certain sum of money, proportioned to the distance or to the work involved? or are they, in addition to their occupation as carriers, to be allowed, simply from the accident of their business (by reason of English law) being necessarily a monopoly, to exercise a direct control over the whole trade of this country, and to regulate, according to their own will and pleasure, the profits of those customers who, owing to the exigencies of their position, are compelled to employ their services for the carriage, not only of produce, but also for the whole of the materials necessary for the production of that produce?

Are they to be allowed to regulate the competition between one town and another, and by a stroke of the pen to make property in one district enormously valuable, whilst at the same time they depreciate it to the same extent in another?

Are they to be allowed to raise the value of lands in America and other corn and meat producing countries of the world, by conferring upon foreign producers the right to use English railways at less rates than the English grower is allowed to use them; and at the same time to depreciate the value of English land in exactly the same proportion as they have enhanced the value of land in other countries?

Are the hundreds of thousands of acres now lying uncultivated in Great Britain and Ireland to remain in their present condition, whilst the country is called upon to assist her sons in emigrating, for the purpose of cultivating the artificially protected lands of foreign countries?

In order to arrive at a correct conclusion—bearing in mind that nothing in these pages will be suggested at variance with any real powers that Railway Companies have had conferred upon them by Act of Parliament—it is necessary to examine their original charters. We find that Parliament originally intended that railways should take the place of the highways, which they supplanted, and on which the cost of carriage was regulated by the distance and the nature of the road. Parliament gave the right to all persons to use the railway with their own engines and trucks, exactly in the same way as they had formerly used the highways with their own horses and carts. It gave the companies the right to charge a certain fixed sum per mile for this user. In case the Railway Companies should find engines and trucks, a certain extra sum per mile was allowed to be charged. It is very difficult to discover in this any evidence that it was intended that Brown of Newcastle should be allowed to use the highway with his engine at a less rate per mile than Smith of York; neither is it easy to see that because Brown and Smith prefer to let the Railway Companies find the engines and the trucks, an equal service for each, and for which the Acts had specified a special and equal mileage charge, that the principle is in any way altered; or, in other words, that because they choose to employ certain common carriers to find locomotives and trucks for their use, that by this act they give these carriers a right to interfere with their respective business, and, in fact, to regulate their profits and losses, as the case may be. Yet the Railway Companies have been drumming into the ears of Parliamentary Committees for many years that this is what they have a right to do, and by sheer effrontery and force of repetition they have at last managed to make certain people believe there is something in their contentions.

They direct the attention of the committee with pride to some particular place that is possibly carrying on an extensive trade, and say that if equal mileage rates were obligatory, that particular trade would stop. Pudlington could not compete with Washington-by-the-Sea. The very obvious answer is, Why should it? Is there any hardship in Inverness not being able to compete with Southampton? If not, where is this competition theory to commence, and where finish?

This question resolves itself into three parts, namely:—

1st. Are the traders and agriculturalists of England entitled individually to the advantages of their geographical position?

2nd. Is it to the advantage of this country, as a nation, that they should have it?

3rd. If not entitled to it, are Railway Companies the proper tribunal to decide how much, if any, they should be allowed to keep?

Now, with regard to No. 1, the matter was decided long before railways were heard of. Clearly every trader then had the exact advantage of his position to an inch, because the cost of transit varied in accordance with the distance the goods were carried by men or horses. One never heard of people in those days going to Parliament to complain that they could not compete with other people who lived somewhere else; but traders very soon discovered for themselves where circumstances permitted trade to be carried on to the most advantage, and there they congregated.

Even now, what decides this question the moment goods leave this country? Clearly the distance and the expense of carriage.

The same rule, as my readers well know, holds good all over the world, with the exception of this country, in which—of all places in the globe!—people are continually exulting in their so-called free trade.

Let us suppose that the coal and iron masters of Northamptonshire and Derbyshire make a railway of their own to London, and that the coal and iron masters of Northumberland and Durham do the same thing. Each body of masters has the exact advantage of its geographical position. How comes it that this advantage is lost or greatly minified because, instead of making separate lines, they both choose to make use of a line which has been sanctioned by Parliament for the use of the general public, and upon which each party has, by Act of Parliament, equal rights?

Now a word or two as to the second question—"Whether it is to the advantage of the country at large that individuals should have the advantage of their natural position." The Railway Companies reply "No; it is greatly for the public good that we should be allowed to bring about an artificial competition, and the public get the benefit of it, and the country is thus enriched."

To test this, let us for argument's sake suppose that England were to make a match to run a dozen men of England against a dozen men of France, the first man reaching the goal on either side to win the match for his respective country.

Suppose that, in addition to this, in order to stimulate the respective runners to do their utmost, money prizes were to be awarded to each runner, according to the position he occupied at the finish of the race. What would be thought of England's chance of winning the match if the best runners were made to start so many yards behind the inferior ones, on the ground that this was only fair and proper, because it gave the inferior men a chance of taking the money prizes? It would certainly do this, and as certainly lose the race for England. In other words, it is tying a weak man to a strong man, and telling them to run a race together.

This brings us to the third question, viz.:—"That if the traders are not entitled to the advantage of their position, are Railway Companies the proper tribunals to decide how much, if any, they should be allowed to keep?"

We will now for a moment admit that they are

not entitled to the advantages referred to, and that the railway argument is the correct one, and that the strong should be tied to the weak in the race of life.

Let us admit that, for some reason or other, Smith should have his goods carried at a less rate than Brown. The question at once arises, What is the proper tribunal to decide this all-important question, and to say how much advantage should be given to the one over the other? Surely, not the Railway Companies! Surely, by no conceiveable contention can it be proposed that Boards of Directors, who themselves are often heavily engaged in business—often competing with private individuals in the middle or at the end of the monopoly over which they have jurisdiction—should be able to say, "We see that it is very necessary, in the interests of the public and for the sake of creating healthy competition, that goods from the districts where our businesses exist should be carried at a far lower rate per mile than from those in which our competitors' businesses are situated."

Yet this is being done every day. Railway directors, as a matter of fact, do claim to have the right to make a handicap of the trade of this country upon any principle which it may seem proper for them to adopt for the moment.

In other words, they contend that they should compete in a race in which they happen to have the trifling advantage of being able to apportion the different weights to be carried by the competitors. To use the expression of a learned judge when speaking as counsel on this subject, "They wish to make themselves a kind of counterweight to Providence," to which I may add, "especially when Providence has mysteriously separated, by a large extent of country, their businesses from the markets which they wish to reach."

In these remarks there is no intention of saying a word against the honour of railway directors as a body; but it is so very easy, when one has the power to regulate these matters, to bring one's self imperceptibly into a state of mind which is apt to confuse private interests with public interests.

But, however good and honourable railway directors may be, to give them the power of doing what I have described is asking a little too much from human nature, and is also a scandal to the country which allows it. It must be remembered that these gentlemen occupy many and varied positions in life, and are, as a rule, neither better nor worse than other people in a similar position; and that their only claim to wield the enormous powers I have spoken of is derived from the fact of their having taken a certain number of shares in a monopoly created by Parliament, and then obtaining a certain number of votes from the shareholders. Even supposing that the artificial competition theory were the correct one, I think my readers will hardly consider that the above-mentioned qualifications are sufficient to give a few individuals complete command over the entire trade of the British Kingdom.

At present I have merely alluded to the undue preference which railway directors maintain they have a right to give; but there is another and a most insidious mode of defeating the equality sections in Acts of Parliament. I allude to the practice of secretly allowing "drawbacks" to favoured individuals and not to others, viz., that certain people carrying on the same trade, from the same place to the same destination and under the same circumstances, are charged the same rate as their competitors, but that after they have paid it a return of so much per ton is made, and is called a "drawback." The companies do not contend that this is legal, but traders know perfectly well that the practice is adopted most extensively, and in many instances it has given favoured individuals or trading companies almost a perfect monopoly of the trade in certain districts or shipping ports.

The unbountied trader has no power of finding out what takes place, as, owing to the admitted illegality of the transaction, great secrecy and subtlety has to be observed in order that discovery should be avoided. The trader's only remedy is to bring a kind of speculative action, and obtain an order to inspect the company's books. As the company will probably raise a considerable number of points in Judge's Chambers, and appeal upon each one of them as long as they possibly can, the operation of obtaining the order for inspection may last, say, from one to two years, and when it is obtained, the trader may spend the best years of his life without discovering what really exists, but which is altogether untraceable when skilfully disguised and hidden in the labyrinth formed by some few hundred tons of railway books.

SUGGESTED REMEDIES.

1st. That each Railway Company (within their statutory powers) shall be compelled to fix the rates for any description of goods, minerals, or agricultural produce at the rate of so much per ton per mile on their railways and canals.

2nd. That they shall be allowed to vary or graduate the mileage charges according to distance.

3rd. That they shall publish a list showing their mileage charges upon each kind of material or produce (dividing them into long and short distances at their convenience), also stating the difference, if any, between large quantities and small quantities, for single trucks or for full train loads.

4th. That in cases where they are entitled to terminal charges, that the said list shall on every kind of material or produce state the amount of the terminal charge in addition and separately to the mileage charge (always excluding the charge for cartage).

5th. That the said list shall state one uniform

charge per mile for cartage (according to weight) upon each kind of material or produce carted by the said company.

6th. That in case of any drawback, allowance, rebate, or preference, being made to any company, firm, or individual, and not published in the Railway Company's list, that the general manager and accountant shall be individually liable to a fine of a certain sum per month, for every month, or part of a month, in which it can be shown that such drawbacks, etc., have been allowed, unless the said general manager and accountant can prove, within a reasonable time of such drawbacks, etc., having been first granted, that they gave notice in writing to each of their directors, informing them of the existence of such drawbacks, and in that case the directors shall be liable, and not the general manager and accountant.

7th. That any officer of the company, or other person, giving such information as shall lead to a conviction, shall be entitled to half the said fines.

A uniform system of this kind is exactly what Parliament originally intended, and simply carries out the meaning of the different Acts referring to

"Undue Preference," to which I shall subsequently refer.

It will doubtless be urged against the system I have proposed, that the cost of carriage varies with the gradients on different portions of a railway, and that terminal and cartage costs vary in different places; and I am fully aware of these facts.

It is, however, the duty of the Railway Companies to ascertain the cost on the different parts of their system and to strike an average; it is their duty to find out what is a "reasonable charge" for terminals and cartage, and, having done so, to charge the same sum to all traders and producers alike. A coal owner, for instance, does not make any difference in the selling price of that portion of his coals which (from the fact of their being drawn from lower workings) probably cost much more than the others, but he finds out the average cost of the whole, and sells accordingly. My readers will observe in subsequent chapters the terrible use the Railway Companies have made of any discretionary power for the alteration of rates in individual cases. If anything is to be done for the purpose of saving the trade and agriculture of this country, complete uniformity in all railway charges is absolutely indispensable.

Once allow the smallest latitude, and the Railway Companies are the masters of the country. Give them a maximum rate of two shillings per ton and allow them to charge a "reasonable" terminal in addition, and the rate will promptly become £1, if it suits their purpose, they knowing perfectly well that not one person in a thousand dare go to law with them upon any point upon which there can be the smallest doubt.

DRAWBACKS.

Any trader, farmer, or other person, sending traffic over a railway, should have power to make a complaint and claim damages before the Railway Commissioners for alleged drawbacks or allowances made by the said Railway Company to any firm or individual sending similar traffic over the said line, in contravention of the terms of the Equality Acts. That upon such complaint being made, the Railway Commissioners shall have the power to call before them any officer or officers of the

Railway Company, and that they shall state on oath whether any such drawback or allowance is made, and that they shall be liable to cross-examination by the complainant. Also, that the Railway Commissioners shall have power to call before them any person or persons connected with the firms in respect of which the complaint regarding the receipt of drawbacks is made, and that they shall be liable to the same process as the railway officials, but that the cross-examination shall be confined entirely to the points in issue.

SHORT DISTANCE CLAUSES.

MANY of my readers may be unaware of the fact, but it nevertheless remains, that this country is cut up and divided between the different Railway Companies precisely as if it consisted of so many little principalities, with the usual system of frontiers for the crossing, of which its trade is not only heavily taxed, but is delayed in transit.

I may, perhaps, illustrate the position of affairs by giving extracts from a letter of mine which recently appeared in the *Times*. This letter explains the system both in its particular operation and general form, and is as follows :—

"RAILWAY RATES AND FARES.
"*To the Editor of the 'Times.'*

"SIR,

"There is an important branch of the railway rates question which, up to the present time, has not attracted its due amount of public attention. I refer to the short distance clauses of the Railway Acts, which enable the companies, if they so please, to place an almost prohibitive tax on goods or minerals sent from works situate on their systems, and distant, say, from one to a dozen miles, from a junction with another railway on which the owners of the works depend for forwarding their long-through traffic.

"I cannot illustrate my contention better than by mentioning the case of this colliery, which is situate on the Manchester, Sheffield, and Lincolnshire Railway, five and a half miles from the Great Northern and Great Eastern Railways, and one and a half from the Midland.

"Under their short distance clauses, the Manchester, Sheffield, and Lincolnshire Company charge 1s. per ton, and in some cases 1s. 4d. per ton, on through traffic sent to these railways, the maximum rate allowed by law being strictly adhered to. To give an idea of the character of these charges, I may mention that if the Great Northern Company were to charge the same rate per ton per mile for their share of the carriage to London, their rate (instead of the present one of 6s. 11d. per ton) would be 27s. per ton, and the Midland rate would be over £5 per ton. It is notorious that this system of taxation is adopted in a greater or less degree all over England on works which happen to be situate a few hundred yards on the wrong side of a signal post. Competition is impossible. The goods or minerals must pass over the short line; and the only question the Railway Companies ask is, What is the utmost charge we can make under our Acts?

"Now, sir, I do not contend for a moment that Parliament should be asked to reduce or alter any powers of charging which it originally sanctioned, although those powers were obtained many years ago under circumstances vastly different from the existing ones. It must, however, be remembered that the commerce of this kingdom is subjected to competition of the most severe kind, down to the minutest details, and it must surely be beneficial to its interest that a factor bearing so vitally upon the cost of production as the rate of carriage should itself be subjected to the same influence.

"With this object in view, I would suggest that all Railway Companies should have running powers over any lines they come in contact with to all works and private sidings situate within fifteen miles of the point of junction. If this were so, the carriage over the short distances, instead of being absolutely in the hands of a single company, would be competed for by all other companies interested. The company carrying the long-through traffic would say to the short line, 'If you insist on your *maximum* rate and refuse to carry at a reasonable one, we shall send our own engines for the traffic, and pay you for the use of your railway.'

"Doubtless, many Railway Companies will contend that, owing to the crowded state of their lines, they have no room to spare; but this argument will not hold water. The traffic on the lines must be dealt with, and whether worked by engines marked with the initial letters of one company or another does not matter.

"But, sir, the powers I am proposing to give to Railway Companies are rights which all private traders possess. All traders are entitled to run their own locomotives on railways. The same Act of Parliament which authorizes the Manchester, Sheffield, and Lincolnshire Company to charge the rates I have referred to, gives power to the trader to run his own engines at five-eighths of a penny per ton per mile.

"I merely mention this to show that it must be far more convenient to Railway Companies to have the short traffic thrown open to competition among themselves than to incur the inconvenience of being inundated with private engines. The arbitrary use some companies are making of their powers, coupled with the depressed state of trade, makes it certain that private engines will be used to a considerable extent, or a change in the law must take place in the direction I have pointed out."

It is difficult to understand how Parliament ever came to give such powers as those alluded to, except upon the assumption that any abuse of them could be corrected by the public themselves in making use of their own engines.

Now, let us see how the company referred to in the *Times* becomes entitled to charge one shilling per ton for carriage over a mile and a half to their railway. It is by virtue of the South Yorkshire Transfer Act, 1864, section 17, which states, "That in respect of all coal, coke, culm, or charcoal, conveyed upon the South Yorkshire Railway from pits situate within six miles of the point of junction of the South Yorkshire with any other railway to any place for consumption within a distance of twenty-five miles from such point of junction, the company shall be entitled to a maximum charge not exceeding ninepence per ton; and in respect of all other coal, coke, culm, or charcoal, the company shall be entitled to a minimum rate of one shilling per ton, irrespective of distance, etc."

This section, whether intentionally or not, gives

the company power to charge ninepence per ton for removing coal to any junction within six miles, such coal to be consumed within a distance of twenty-five miles of that junction; but if, on the other hand, the coal is going to a distant market (with the carriage of which the company working the short distance has nothing whatever to do), then they have the power of charging an extra twenty-five per cent. or one shilling per ton. This entirely reverses the principle contended for by Railway Companies, viz., that the rates for short distances should be higher per mile than for long ones. These maximum charges are, however, invariably exacted, and really amount to a crushing tax.

Now, the same Act in section 13 provides for the protection of the coalowner, by giving him the use of the railway at so much per ton per mile. It states, "for all coal, coke, culm, and charcoal, conveyed upon such railways, the sum of five-eighths of a penny per ton per mile for the use of the railway; and if drawn or propelled by engine or other power provided by the company, an additional sum per ton per mile, not exceeding two-eighths of a penny."

It is, therefore, perfectly clear that the coal-owner has the same right to run his engines as the company have to charge their maximum rate of one shilling.

Let us see how this would work out. The mile and a half referred to, at the rate of five-eighths of a penny per mile, would come to a fraction under a penny per ton, and allowing another penny per ton for the use of the engine, the net gain to the colliery would be about tenpence per ton. When I remind my readers that many collieries raise from one thousand to two thousand tons daily, and taking into consideration the fact that the profits on coal working during the last six or seven years averaged over the whole of England have certainly not amounted to threepence per ton, I need say no more to show how certain it is that the coalowners would adopt this mode of sending their produce if they were allowed, and what an enormous saving would arise.

But it is just at this point that the Railway Companies step in and say "No; it is quite right that we should exact the maximum rate, because section 17 gives us the power to do so. But you must not take advantage of section 13, which enables you to carry your coal at twopence instead of our carrying it at one shilling, as it will be inconvenient to our traffic to have your engines running on our line; and because of this inconvenience, you must be good enough to allow us to tax you tenpence per ton."

If the right is insisted on, the Railway Companies are quite equal to the occasion; for they refuse to quote rates from the junction, and likewise put every possible impediment in the way—systematically playing into each other's hands. To sum the matter up, they claim to have the right to charge the utmost farthing they are entitled to under one section of an Act, and of confiscating, on the ground of their own convenience, all that the public can claim under another.

It is difficult to say whether the system referred to is more injurious to the trade of the country or to the Railway Companies themselves. The loss, between the two, is simply enormous, as in order to secure these heavy taxes (which it would be a misnomer to term " rates "), no sooner has the Railway Company (carrying the short initial distance) taken up the trucks than it has to shunt them off again into exchange sidings, connecting the through

D

line. This entails a large staff and other expenses to the companies, of an entirely unnecessary and unproductive nature; whilst to the trader it means continual delay to his traffic and his trucks in the outward and (to the latter) in the homeward journeys, together with the loss occasioned to his trucks by being subjected to constant and wholly unnecessary shunting, in which they probably receive more injury than in all the proper service of the journey.

The companies also lose heavily by the slow process of crushing the various kinds of industries affected, which would otherwise bring "grist" to their "mill"; but this loss, concealed as it is under the illusion of heavy rates, and spread over the whole of these vast monopolies, is comparatively lightly borne. It is, however, far otherwise with people who have invested the whole or a large portion of their capital in the particular works affected, who, together with their workmen, feel the effect in a form which is fearfully concentrated and intense. The absurdity of the situation is complete, when one recollects that the only country in which this kind of thing exists is in "Free-trading" England. It is only here that, for the use of a few hundred yards of the country's great highways of commerce, which happen to be situated on "the wrong side of the signal post," a trader can be taxed in a sum sufficient to make the difference between fortune and bankruptcy as compared with his rival, whose works are situated a few yards on the right side.

Whether the trade of this country is in a sufficiently prosperous state to be able to bear this burden, I must leave to the reflection of my readers.

SUGGESTED REMEDIES.

THE new Railway Act should decree that, for the purposes of promoting competition, in any case in which a Railway Company charges (under its short distance clauses) for the carriage of coal, iron, agricultural produce, or any other substance, whatsoever sums which amount to more than its ordinary maximum mileage charges from any works or sidings to any junction connecting the aforesaid line with other railways, that it shall be lawful for any of the said other Railway Companies to go before the Railway Commissioners, and, upon making an affidavit of the said facts, to ask the commissioners, and that the commissioners shall have power to grant to the said Railway Companies running powers to the works or sidings referred to, on their paying such toll to the said company (whose line is used) as Parliament has already decreed shall be paid by private individuals for the use of their own engines.

2nd. That from all such works and sidings before mentioned, the Railway Companies shall be compelled (in all cases where they can be proved to have charged more than their maximum mileage charges) to give to the owners of the works, or the senders of the goods from the sidings referred to, every facility for the running of their own engines to the exchange sidings of the receiving companies. That the receiving companies shall be bound to give all facilities, and to treat the traffic in the same way as if carried by the company upon whose line the works and sidings are situated.

That for any contravention of the said Act, the owner of the works, or the forwarder of the goods from the sidings referred to, shall have power to bring an action before the Railway Commissioners, and, if successful, to recover such damages as they may consider he has incurred. And that the commissioners be empowered to restrain by injunction the company from continuing the illegal practice complained of, and to punish by fine. That upon action being taken, the commissioners to have the power to send for any officer or officers of the companies complained of, and that they shall be liable to cross-examination by the complainants, but only in respect of the matter at issue.

SELECT COMMITTEE ON RAILWAY RATES AND FARES, 1881.

At the first meeting of the committee the Hon. Evelyn Ashley was appointed chairman on the motion of a railway director, a counter-motion "that Mr. Samuelson do take the chair" being defeated by one vote.

The committee consisted to a very large extent of railway directors, who adopted the practice already alluded to, viz. they sat in judgment on themselves. Thus, if a member of the public gave evidence against the action of any particular Railway Company, he had the satisfaction of knowing that he was probably complaining to the very person who, as chairman or director of the company, was directly (or through his agents) perpetrating the acts alluded to. This was the kind of tribunal appointed to try not only the issue between the traders and the general public on the one hand, and the Railway Companies on the other, but an issue which involved the future of England's trade and its prosperity as a nation. So far as I am aware, there was no general invitation or notice given to persons throughout the kingdom that the committee was sitting, and that, if necessary, they could be heard ; but the evidence of the public seemed chiefly confined to certain individuals who happened to be personally acquainted with members of the committee. These gentlemen, after being examined in chief in a rather hurried manner, and subjected to continual interruptions, were afterwards immediately cross-examined by the railway directors, who were, of course, in possession of the most minute facts relating to the matters complained of, and of any other facts which could by the aid of experienced skill be made to throw a complexion on the matter adverse to the witnesses' contentions. But if England was not ransacked for evidence on behalf of the public, it was thoroughly well worked on the other side. The gigantic railway machine was set in motion all over the kingdom, and any evidence which could possibly help the companies was given by gentlemen who were not only nearly all skilled parliamentary witnesses, but who had this advantage over the public, viz. that they knew the particulars on both sides of the case down to the smallest *minutiæ*, and could either give or withhold them, as occasion required. The general managers, or traffic managers (and sometimes both), connected with almost every line in the kingdom of any importance were brought up one after the other, and gave lengthy and exhaustive evidence. Indeed, the mass of statements vouchsafed had rather a bewildering effect, which effect, however, is not regarded as an altogether unfavourable factor by Railway Companies when appearing before committees for the purpose of maintaining the *status quo ante.*

One would have supposed that after all these gentlemen had been patiently heard out, the evidence was finished. But not so! The most eminent counsel (all specially retained by different Railway Companies) were then invited to give their views on the question, and it followed, as a matter of course, that their views were *not* very antagonistic to the railway side of the question. One of them, on being asked who invited him to give evidence, replied that he did so "at the request of a certain honourable member of the committee," which honourable member was chairman or director of no less than six Railway Companies.

Counsel were allowed to give their views on cases in which they had been engaged between the Railway Companies and the public, and to give evidence as to facts which the Railway Companies in their exhaustive evidence (and who were the only people responsible for the truth) had for some reason chosen to avoid. I regret to say that some of this evidence was gravely inaccurate and misleading. However, when these gentlemen had finished, a Mr. T. H. Farrer was introduced, who turned out to be no less a personage than the Permanent Secretary of the Board of Trade. Now the Board of Trade has always been looked upon as a kind of judicial buffer (although not a very effective one) between the public and the railways, and the evidence before the committee positively teemed with suggestions in the direction of increasing its powers and usefulness in this capacity. It was, therefore, just a little startling to find the Permanent Secretary of that institution giving evidence mainly devoted to show how in his opinion the public were greatly benefited by unequal rates ; but when subsequently that gentleman considered it his duty to send to the *Fortnightly Review* a most elaborate article epitomizing all the railway arguments on this subject, the effect was still more surprising. Here was a distinct issue between two classes (comprising the whole of the community) and a public servant occupying almost a judicial position in respect of matters relative to that issue, not only giving evidence on one side, but rushing into print to try to substantiate it to the British public with all the weight which his official position afforded. Not only had the Railway Companies provided him with his arguments, but apparently with his facts ; for otherwise it is difficult to understand how he could have obtained so exhaustive a knowledge of the matters connected with the different disputes between the railways and the public. Considering the whole of the circumstances, and how important it is that the public should have every confidence in the Board of Trade, it might have been expected that the Government would either have removed him to some other department or have asked him for his resignation ; but they apparently thought otherwise, as he was kept in the same position, and shortly afterwards rewarded with a baronetcy.

In the year 1882, at the close of the evidence, a number of very antagonistic draft reports were drawn up by different members of the committee. The voting (as in the case of the appointment of the chairman) was very close, but eventually to all intents and purposes the railway directors won the day, and a report was adopted, to some of whose salient features I will shortly refer.

Before doing so, I must state that the great weight of railway evidence was given with the one object of impressing the committee with the idea that unequal rating was a necessity, and that anything like a mileage system was out of the question. This was the real issue involved, and the key to the whole railway position.

On this issue (as in preceding chapters I have pointed out) depends the question whether railway directors are to be endowed with powers greater than those possessed by constitutional monarchs, or whether they are to take their place with the ordinary trader, and be paid in proportion to the work they do.

Now, before referring to what the committee

said on the subject, I will first state what the law says. Previous to 1844, there was no general law relating to preference, but special provisions were inserted in each Act, authorizing the construction of the railway. As an example, let us take 6 Will. IV. c. 75, s. 137 (1836), which states—

"That the aforesaid rates and tolls to be taken by virtue of this Act shall at all times be charged equally and after the same rate per ton per mile throughout the whole of the said railways, in respect of the same descriptions of articles, matters, or things ; and that no reduction or advance in the said rates and tolls shall either directly or indirectly be made partially or in favour of or against any particular person or company, or be confined to any particular part of the said railway, but that every such reduction or advance of rates and tolls upon any particular kind or description of article, matter, or thing, shall extend to and take place throughout the whole and every part of the said railways upon and in respect of the same description of articles, matters, and things thereon, anything to the contrary thereof in any wise notwithstanding."

In 1844 the Railway Clauses Consolidation Act was passed, and contained an equality clause.

In 1854 an Act known as Cardwell's Act was passed. Section 2 requires every Railway Company to give all reasonable facilities for the conveyance of traffic, etc., and says, "No such company shall make or give any undue or unreasonable preference or advantage to or in favour of any particular person or company or any particular description of traffic in any respect whatsoever, nor shall any such company subject any particular person or any particular description of traffic to any undue or unreasonable prejudice or disadvantage in any respect whatsoever."

From this, reader, it is quite clear that when Parliament sanctioned the making of railways it did not intend that the corn and the meat produced in England should be carried at a high rate, in order that the corn and the meat produced in America should be carried at a low one; neither did it intend that the directors of the said railways should, *ipso facto*, become so many little kings.

However, let us now see what the report of the Select Committee says on the subject. Under that portion of the report which relates to "fixing rates" it says—

The form which the proposal for a fixed standard of charges has usually taken is 'equal,' viz. a charge for each class of goods and passengers in proportion to the distance for which they are carried. This point was much urged before the Royal Commission, and is so effectually disposed of by their report that it seem scarcely necessary to dwell upon it further. But it appears in the evidence of some of the witnesses before this committee, and it may, therefore, be desirable to state shortly why it is so impracticable.

Taking the Act of 1836 and the subsequent legislation referred to into consideration, this statement forms an excellent illustration of the mode in which railway directors, by the aid of Royal Commissions and Select Committees (of which they not only form the chief part but provide the greater part of the evidence), manage at last by the simple reiteration of the reports of those bodies to impart to their own wishes and ideas a kind of quasi-legal embodification, which, although in direct variance with the law of the land, they ever afterwards look upon and refer to as to so many Acts of Parliament.

In this case, however, their usual astuteness is not shown, because instead of simply relying on the report of the Royal Commission, they proceed to give their reasons. These reasons are set forth in three paragraphs marked A, B, C, and for convenience I will, in the first instance, deal with B and C.

"B" states as a reason why an equal mileage system is impracticable that—

It would prevent Railway Companies from making perfectly fair arrangements for carrying at a lower rate than usual goods brought in larger and constant quantities, or for carrying for long distances at a lower rate than short distances.

"C" states—

It would compel a company to carry for the same rate over a line which has been very expensive in construction, or which, from gradients or otherwise, is very expensive in working at the same rate at which it carries over less expensive lines.

In answer to these statements, I must refer my readers to the "Suggested Remedies" mentioned under the chapter "Undue Preference." They will find that in advocating equal mileage rates, I have foreseen the very trivial difficulties raised by "B" and "C," and have stated how they can be provided for.

The marrow of the railway argument is, however, to be found in "A," which states—

It would prevent Railway Companies from lowering their fares and rates, so as to compete with traffic by sea, by canal, or by a shorter or otherwise cheaper railway, and would thus deprive the public of the benefit of competition, and the company of a legitimate source of profit.

This being interpreted means—

1st. That if "equal mileage" charges are enforced, the Railway Companies will be prevented from taking advantage of those traders or agriculturists who happen to be at their mercy.

2nd. That they will be prevented from taxing the trade or produce of the aforesaid traders and agriculturists sufficiently to repay them for carrying other traffic at unremunerative rates, such unremunerative rates being necessary for the pious purpose of ruining people who compete with them by canal or by sea.

3rd. The report would have us believe that the sea and canal traffic being ruined, and the whole trade thrown into the hands of the Railway Companies, the public will thus receive "the benefit of competition." I do not consider it necessary to add one word of further comment with respect to this paragraph, but will conclude with an illustration of the "benefit of competition" enjoyed by the public under the present system. Before the opening of the Great Western Railway to the west of Plymouth, vegetables from Cornwall were carried by sea to Bristol, and from there by rail to London, at 50s. per ton. On the opening of the railway, the company carried at 25s. a ton until the steamers were starved off, and the company then at once put back the rate to 50s. per ton, the judicious application of the power appertaining to seventy-two millions of capital making short work of the shipping interests and the public's competitive route!

Having dealt sufficiently with the report of the committee on this subject, I will now proceed to state what that report would have been had there been one or two less railway directors on the committee. It is embodied in the following passages of Mr. Barclay's draft report :—

"The business of a railway is to carry traffic ; and when by carrying it at an unremunerative rate,—that is, offering a bounty, or by charging excessive rates—that is, imposing a tax,—a Railway Company diverts traffic or production from the natural and consequently the cheapest channels, it must thereby increase the general cost of commodities to the consumer."

CANALS.

Under this head, the report states that—

Serious charges have been made by traders and Canal Companies as against Railway Companies, in respect of the working of canals owned by them, or of which they control the navigation. Cases have been adduced where Railway Companies having acquired possession or control of a canal have ceased to work it, or allowed it to fall into disrepair, or charged excessive tolls, especially in the case of through rates, and that, in consequence, traffic is diverted to the railways, where higher rates are exacted to the injury of traders and the public generally.

Your committee are of opinion that these complaints are not unfounded. A Railway Company, owning or controlling a canal, may think it profitable to lose the revenue of the canal in expectation of deriving a greater revenue from the railway to which it is a competitor, and where the canal forms part of a through competing route, it is obviously to its interest, as a general rule, to discourage through traffic. Transportation can frequently be effected more cheaply by canal navigation than by railway, particularly where the traffic consists of heavy goods of little value, or where speed is not of importance. Your committee are therefore of opinion that it is impolitic that Railway Companies should have the control, either directly or indirectly, of canal navigation; and that where canals are already under the control of Railway Companies, Parliament should endeavour to insure their use to the fullest extent.

Subsequently the committee recommend that Parliament should not sanction any further control direct or indirect, of canal navigation by a Railway Company; but taking into consideration the fact that nearly the whole of the canals in England are either bought, controlled, or are working under agreements with the Railway Companies, this recommendation (as Professor Hunter remarks in his able treatise on the report of the committee) is very like "recommending the groom to lock the stable door after the horse has been stolen." Notwithstanding that a factor in English trade affecting its welfare to so great an extent as the canal navigation of this country has, by the admission of the committee, either been destroyed or improperly converted by the Railway Companies to their own use, the report proceeds to state—

> That on the whole of the evidence they acquit the companies of any grave dereliction of their duty to the public;

and it may be interesting to my readers to know how this verdict was arrived at. Ten members voted for, and nine against it. Of the majority seven were railway directors, so that out of a committee of twenty-seven members (if one accepts the votes of those gentlemen who were on their trial) only three are responsible for the decision.

After reading the evidence which I give in the ensuing chapter, my readers will have an opportunity of judging not only of the worth of this acquittal, but of the value of the whole report.

EXTRACTS FROM THE EVIDENCE OF THE TRADING PUBLIC BEFORE SELECT COMMITTEE.

In reading the trade reports of this country, my readers must have been struck with the fact that although the volume is apparently immense, it is nearly always described as of an unprofitable nature. This is explained by the fact that nearly the whole of our trade is either in the hands of, or is controlled by, the Railway Companies, and that they are authorized by law to charge such enormous maximum rates that if they were to be exacted on traffic passing over long distances, the whole trade of the country and the railways themselves would be brought to a standstill at one and the same time. For these distances, therefore, they charge what the trade will bear, which means that having the traders and agriculturists completely at their mercy, they tax them practically to the extent of their profits, taking advantage of the fact that persons having large sums invested in their business will carry them on for a lengthened period at no profit, and sometimes at a loss, rather than throw up the sponge, which would mean at once a loss of nearly their entire capital. For short distances the Railway Companies charge not only their maximum rates, but, in many cases, sums amounting to two hundred or three hundred per cent. in excess of their rates. The principle of exacting " what the trade will bear " is still adhered to, regardless of the fact that the illegality involved in charging more than the extreme rate sanctioned by law amounts to an act of robbery towards the person so charged.

Professor Hunter.

Prof. Hunter. The first witness called was MR. W. A. HUNTER; and I will now give extracts from that gentleman's evidence with regard to railway charges in excess of maximum or legal charges.

"Q. You are a barrister-at-law, professor of jurisprudence at University College, and one of the examiners of London University, and to the Inns of Court.

"A. I am.

"Q. You have also been retained by the Farmers' Alliance to prepare and state a case for the committee on their behalf.

"A. I have.

"Q. Will you take the first case of the London and South-Western Company, and give the committee what in you opinion are overcharges by that company in respect of guano and packed manure?

"A. From Petersfield to Nine Elms the charge is 12s. 6d., and the maximum rate is 9s. To Wimbledon the charge is 13s. 4d., and the maximum rate is 8s. 2d. To Woking the charge for manure and guano is 10s. per ton, and the maximum rate 5s. 4d. To Guildford the charge is 9s. 2d., and the maximum rate 4s. 4d. To Witley the charge is 6s. 8d., and the maximum rate 3s. To Haslemere the charge is 5s. 10d., and the maximum 2s. To Liphook the charge is 5s., and the maximum is 1s. 6d.

"Q. In some cases the charges are 300 or 400 per cent. above the charges allowed by the Act?

"A. Yes. Then, taking hops from Nine Elms to Exeter the charge is 55s., and the maximum

PROF. HUNTER.

48s. 6d. To Basingstoke the charge is 25s., and the maximum 11s. 9d. From Petersfield to Exeter the charge is 60s., and the maximum is 36s. For dead poultry and meat, the charge from London to Windsor is 19s. 2d., and the maximum 8s. 6d.

"Q. Now let us take the London and Brighton Railway. Can you give the committee some particulars with regard to potatoes?

"A. For new potatoes the charge from London to Sutton is 6s. 8d., and the maximum is 1s. 9d. From London to Three Bridges the charge is 10s. 10d., and the maximum 3s. 8d. From Horsham to Portsmouth the charge is 16s. 3d., and the maximum is 6s. From Brighton to Portsmouth the actual charge is 15s., and the maximum is 5s. 8d. From Tunbridge Wells to Red Hill the charge is 10s. 10d., and the maximum 3s. 6d. From West Grinstead to Hastings the charge is 17s. 6d., and the maximum is 6s. 8d. Now, taking the London and Brighton Company's trade rates for meat, poultry, eggs, butter, and vegetables (of course, I can only compare the charge with the maximum charge for goods), they have a scale; and I have taken the distance at twenty, forty, fifty, and eighty miles. At a distance of twenty miles they charge 20s. per ton. The maximum rate for eggs is 3s. 4d., and the maximum rate for other articles is 6s. 8d. Then at forty miles they charge 30s., the maximum rate for eggs being 6s. 8d., and for meat 13s. 4d. At fifty miles they charge 40s. per ton; the maximum for eggs is 8s. 4d., and for other things 16s. 8d. At eighty miles they charge 60s. per ton; for eggs the maximum is 13s. 4d., and for meat 26s. 8d.

PROF. HUNTER.

"Q. Will you give the committee some examples of charges upon the London, Chatham, and Dover Railway?

"A. From Dover to Shepherd's Well, where manure is sent in quantities of not less than four tons, the charge is 2s. 11d. per ton, and if carried in quantities of less than four tons, 3s. 4d. per ton, the legal maximum being 9d. per ton. Then, from Canterbury to Faversham the charge is 2s. 11d. in quantities of not less than four tons, and 3s. 4d. in quantities of less than four tons, the maximum rate being 1s. 3d. per ton. Then from Faversham to Sittingbourne there is the same rate, 2s. 11d. per ton for four tons or over, and 3s. 4d. for under four tons, the maximum rate being 10½d. Now, as regards guano and packed manures, from Favers-

PROF. HUNTER. ham to Whitstable, in quantities of less than two tons, the charge is 3*s.* 4*d.* per ton, and the maximum rate is 9*d.* From Sevenoaks to Blackfriars the charge for hops is 21*s.* 8*d.*, and the maximum rate is 8*s.* 7*d.* From Canterbury to London the maximum rate is 20*s.* 7*d.*, and the charge is 35*s.* From London to Sevenoaks the rate for furniture carried at owner's risk is 24*s.* 2*d.*, and the charge at the company's risk is 35*s.* 10*d.*, the maximum being 8*s.* From London to Canterbury, at owner's risk, the rate is 56*s.* 2*d.*, at the company's risk 71*s.* 8*d.*, the maximum being 20*s.* From Faversham to Chatham the charge is 20*s.* 10*d.* at owner's risk, and 28*s.* 4*d.* at the company's risk, and the maximum rate is 6*s.*

"Q. Will you be good enough to give the committee some examples of the charges made by the South-Eastern Company.

"A. From Tunbridge Wells to Wadhurst for fruit the charge is 8*s.* 4*d.* per ton; for dead game, etc., 10*s.* 10*d.*; for furniture, 21*s.* 8*d.*; the maximum rate being 2*s.* for any class of goods. To Hastings for fruit, etc., the charge is 15*s.* 10*d.* per ton; for dead game, 19*s.* 7d.; and for furniture, 39*s.* 2*d.*; the maximum rate being 9*s.* 4d. Then, from Hastings to Robertsbridge the charge is 10s. 5d. for fruit, 14s. 2d. for dead game, and 28s. 4d. for furniture, the maximum rate being 4s. 4d.

"Q. Do you think there should be a penalty for overcharging?

"A. I think that when a Railway Company charges any person higher than the charge in the rate book, they ought to be subject to a penalty.

"Q. Railway Companies claim a penalty against passengers in the meantime attempting to travel for less than the company is entitled to?

"A. Yes. If I travel on a first-class carriage with a second-class ticket, they ask for a penalty against me."

From lack of space I have been compelled to confine myself to a comparatively small number of Professor Hunter's instances of rates in excess of the legal ones, and shall, from the mass of similar evidence, merely quote a few instances here and there given by other people, in order to show that the system alluded to in the South is in force nearly all over the kingdom, and sufficient to prove that the law is openly and audaciously set at defiance.

Professor Hunter was, of course, cross-examined

by the railway directors; not, however, for the purpose of disputing his figures, but in order to show that under certain circumstances the companies are entitled to terminal charges in excess of their maximum rates, such terminal charges including the loading or unloading of goods, or covering them from the effects of the weather, and for which they are entitled to make "a reasonable charge." I commend to the reflection of my readers the suggestion that the excess of the actual rates to the legal ones in the instances I have enumerated can be explained by "a reasonable terminal charge." For instance, can it be claimed that the charge for the carriage of a ton of eggs for a distance of eighty miles, fixed by law at a sum not exceeding 13$s.$ 4$d.$, can be raised to £3 by the company rendering assistance in putting the baskets into and taking them out of the train? If any doubt should still remain on the subject, let me give some other instances mentioned by Professor Hunter with respect to the South-Eastern Companies' rates, which are as follow:—

PROF. HUNTER (*continued*).

"Taking, first, lime and manure in bulk, in quantities over four tons, where loading and unloading have to be done by the parties, from

Hastings to Robertsbridge, the charge is 3s. 4d., and the maximum rate is 9d. Then from Hastings to Rye the charge is 3s. 5d., and the maximum rate is 2s. 3½d.

"Q. Are these station to station rates?

"A. Yes.

"Q. And it is provided that the consignee and consignor have to load and unload?

"A. Yes. There is no question of terminals.

"Q. Is there no question of covering, and so on?

"A. No. Then, the charge from Tunbridge Wells to Battle is 3s. 5d., and the maximum rate is 1s. 7½d. From Ashford to Staplehurst it is 3s. 9d., and the maximum rate would be 1s. 9d."

Here then we have rates varying from two hundred to three hundred per cent. in excess of the legal ones, for which the company cannot even claim the excuse that they are put to the expense of finding a porter to assist in loading or unloading, or that in order to protect the goods from the weather they give for a few hours the use of a tarpaulin!

Having, I think, now clearly demonstrated that the Railway Companies are converting to their own use in a wholesale manner money belonging to the trading and agricultural classes, I will now proceed to deal with the dictatorship exercised over those classes by railway directors through the medium of "preferential rates."

[Prof. Hunter (continued).]

"Q. Can you tell the committee the charge for hops from Sittingbourne to London?

"A. From Sittingbourne to London the charge is 36s. 8d., including delivery.

"Q. As against 25s. from Flushing?

"A. Yes.

"Q. What are the respective distances?

"A. The distance from Sittingbourne to London is sixty miles, and the distance from Flushing is all the additional distance across the sea to Queenborough.

"Q. But how much further is it from Sittingbourne to Queenborough?

"A. About four miles. From Paris to the Bricklayers' Arms, the charge is 28s.; and from Boulogne to Bricklayers' Arms, the charge is 17s. 6d.

"Q. What port does that traffic come through?

"A. From Boulogne to Folkestone; and to compare with that I take English hops from Ashford, which is fifty-four miles, and the charge

is 35s. per ton. I have a list of other stations PROF. HUNTER.
with which I will not trouble the committee, but
will hand it in with the appendix. From Boulogne
to Folkestone, it will be remembered, there are two
tranships. They would have to load at the
steamer, and unload and load at the railway; and
there would be wharfage.

"Q. Is there any competition from Ashford to
London?

"A. There is not. At present the Railway
Company may lower its rates for particular traffic
at a particular place, and at the same time charge
very much higher rates at different portions of their
line. Take the instance of the foreign produce
which I have mentioned. The companies find it
profitable, I assume, to carry foreign produce at the
rates I have quoted. If you insisted on equality,
then they would require to lower their rates to the
home producer, or to raise the rates to the foreign
producer, and the probability is that the home
producer would gain materially by the process.

"Q. Will you state to the committee what you
consider the sound principle in the public interest
in regard to competition?

"A. I consider the sound principle is, that

PROF. HUNTER.

goods should go by the route, whether by land or sea, which is naturally the best and, therefore, the cheapest. For example, take the case of the Denaby Colliery, which I mentioned on the last occasion. Here is a colliery four miles from a seaport. Another colliery is twenty miles from that seaport.* The Railway Companies make the same charge to both collieries. Now, if that is a reasonable charge for the colliery which is nearest the seaport, it follows that the directors are giving a bounty to the more distant collieries out of the pockets of the shareholders. On the other hand, if the distant collieries are charged a reasonable price, then it follows that an illegitimate tax is imposed upon the nearer colliery in the nature of a protective duty in favour of the more distant collieries.

"Q. In the one case the company offers a bounty to the colliery, and in the other it imposes a protective tax?

"A. That is so. At present Railway Com-

---

* The Denaby Colliery is not four miles from a seaport, but about four and a half miles from a junction with a railway leading to a seaport. The principle is, however, in no way affected, as the Railway Company charged for the carriage over this distance the same rate as from collieries situated more than twenty miles distant.

panies are governed by the law; but they may vary the rates in any way they please, until some person goes to the expense of taking them before the Railway Commissioners. Now, it seems to me worthy of consideration whether the law might not require the approbation of the Railway Commissioners in advance, in order to protect the community against unequal rating; in other words, the law might require equal rates, leaving it to the Railway Companies to propose inequalities upon any part of their system, they first obtaining the sanction of the Railway Commissioners to those inequalities. The sanction of the commissioners would be granted if, by reason of guaranteed quantities, or of longer distances, or of special difficulties in working, or of any other matters affecting the cost of conveyance, it was reasonable that an inequality should be made.

Prof. Hunter.

"Q. You would have equal rates as a rule without any exception, except with the sanction of the commissioners?

" A. Certainly."

Mr. Samuel Rowlandson, examined :—

" Q. You are a farmer, residing near Darlington?

MR. ROW-LANDSON.

"A. Newton Darrell, Darlington.

"Q. What bodies have asked you to come and give evidence?

"A. The South Durham and North Yorkshire Chambers of Agriculture, and I was also asked at a meeting of farmers held at Darlington last Monday.

"Q. Is there a strong feeling in your district against the system of charging by the Railway Companies?

"A. It is very strong indeed.

"Q. Will you give the committee some example of the preference given to foreign cattle first?

"A. The rate is given to me by some large cattle dealers. From Newcastle to Manchester for foreign cattle in a small waggon, is £2 4s. 3d., and English cattle £3 7s. per waggon with a corresponding difference in a large waggon. The sheep rates from Newcastle to Manchester are, for foreign sheep £2 4s. 3d., and English sheep £2 14s. For seven imported cattle in a small waggon from Newcastle to Wakefield the charge is £1 11s. 6d., and for seven English in a similar waggon is £2 12s. From West Hartlepool to Mirfield the charge in four ton loads for foreign barley is 8s. 9d., and the charge for four ton loads of home-grown barley is 10s. 10d. and two tons of home-grown at 18s. 4d. From Tyne Dock, Newcastle, to York, two tons of imported grain are charged at 7s. 6d., and two tons of English grain at 11s. 8d.

"Q. Now, as to inconsistencies on the charge for the carriage of grain between different points on the North-Eastern system. What is the carriage of grain from Sunderland to Seaham to different points?

"A. The rate is 10s. per ton from Leeds, Staddlethorpe, Timberborough, and Malton.

"Q. Then what is the carriage from Hull?

"A. From Hull to Tyne Dock, Newcastle, it is 8s. 4d., although for a considerably longer distance.

"Q. Then they carry to the Tyne Dock, Newcastle, for 8s. 4d., although the distance is forty miles greater than some of the other distances?

"A. Yes, that is so. The carriage for imported oil cake from Newcastle to Darlington in four ton loads is 5s. 10d. per ton, and of home-made cake 6s. 8d. per ton. The charge for a truck of grazing steers from Richmond to Berwick-on-Tweed is 61s. or 63s., and the distance 122 miles; and from Tebay to Berwick-on-Tweed or rather Tweedmouth, the charge is £2 6s. 9d.

MR. ROW-
LANDSON.

"Q. And in the one case the company charge £2 13s. for carrying 122 miles, and in the other they charge £2 6s. 9d. for carrying 160 miles?

"A. They charge £2 6s. 9d. for about 160 miles, as against £3 or £3 3s. for about 122.

"Q. Do these foreign cattle get the preference in regard to home cattle?

"A. That is one point the cattle dealers complain of very much indeed—that the foreign cattle are placed in the through fast trains, whereas that accommodation is refused to the home stock.

"Q. In those rates for cattle between Newcastle and Manchester there is a difference of £1 2s. 9d. per truck?

"A. Yes.

"Q. Is there any circumstance to justify that difference which affect the cost of transit?

"A. Not that I am aware of.

"Q. All things are equal, except that one is foreign and the other is home produce?

"A. Yes.

"Q. The foreign producer is now a competitor in the English market?

"A. Yes.

"Q. So that although it may be quite correct,

as the honourable member for South Durham said, that the railways are right in doing the best they can for their shareholders, yet is not this establishing an inequality between these two classes of competitors?

MR. ROW-LANDSON.

"A. There is no doubt of it. *It is putting a tax of so much per acre on our productions.*

"Q. It does not affect the individual competitor, but the whole district.

"A. It affects the whole production.

MAXIMUM RATES.

"Q. Can you tell the committee what is the charge of the North-Eastern Railway on artificial manure between Stockton and Darlington?

"A. The charge on the four ton loads and upwards is 3s. 4d. per ton.

"Q. What is the distance?

"A. The distance is 11½ miles; that is to say, about 3½d. per ton.

"Q. For two ton loads, how much is the charge?

"A. Five shillings per ton—that is about fivepence per ton per mile. For less than two tons 6s. 3d. per ton, which is about 6¼d. per mile.

MR. ROW-
LANDSON.

"Q. I suppose a good many farmers do not exceed two tons of manure?

"A. The great bulk of the farmers in our neighbourhood do not require more than two tons of any special kind of manure.

"Q. Have you any idea what is the maximum limit of charge by the North-Eastern Railway for manure?

"A. I believe that it is 1*d.* per ton over twenty miles and 1½*d.* per ton under twenty miles.

"Q. Then, if your impression is correct, the North-Eastern Company is, for small lots, charging more than four times its maximum rate?

"A. Yes."

MR. THOMAS GARNETT, examined:—

"Q. You are a stuff merchant at Bradford, and a member of the Chamber of Commerce at Bradford?

"A. I am.

"Q. And chairman of the Railway Committee of that body?

"A. Yes.

"Q. Are you of opinion that the great and increasing interests of the worsted and woollen interests suffer from the inequalities of the rates of railway carriage?

"A. I am.

"Can you give the committee the rates of carriage from Manchester and Bradford respectively, for exportation only?

"A. The rate from Manchester to London is 25s. a ton. The rate from Bradford to London is 35s. per ton. The distance from Manchester to London is 182 miles, and from Bradford to London 188 to 190 miles.

"Q. Then, for this small difference of distance, there is a difference of 10s. per ton as between Bradford and Manchester for shipping carriage?

"A. Yes.

"Q. Can you give the rates on your goods from Manchester and Bradford to London for the home trade?

"A. From Manchester the rate is 40s., and from Bradford to London it is 43s. 4d.

"Q. Then, in point of fact, the home consumer pays sixty per cent. more than the foreign buyer from Bradford?

"A. If the home consumer bought from Bradford, and the shipping goods went from Manchester to exactly the same extent, the foreign purchaser would get an advantage of exactly sixty per cent. in carriage over the home consumer."

MR. ISAAC BANKS, examined :—

"Q. I believe you are manager for the Clyde Shipping Company?

"A. Yes, I am. That company have steamers running from Cork to Waterford, Belfast, Dublin, Glasgow, and Greenock ; also a line running from Cork to the south-west coast of Cork and Kerry.

"Q. You were recently employed at Cork as local agent for the Great Western Company of England?

"A. Yes. Before then I was twenty-one years with the traffic department of the Limerick Railway.

"Q. Then you understand all the railway questions, we may assume ?

"A. I commenced as a boy, and was traffic manager of the line when I left them.

"Q. Did you try to get upon the Great Southern and Western Company, to examine their rate books?

"A. I did. On the 3rd of January last I applied at the Cork goods office for some rates and permission to see the rate book, but the manager in charge informed me it was contrary to the Railway Company's regulations to allow me to inspect them. That was the head manager of the goods department.

"Q. How were you able to get the rates?

"A. I sent an assistant from my office with a copy of the Railway and Canal Traffic Act. Even after that I could not get the rate books for examination.

"Q. He declines still?

"A. Yes, my lord.

"Q. Notwithstanding that you referred the manager to the Act?

"A. Notwithstanding that I produced the Act of Parliament for his inspection.

"Q. Do the railways running into Cork encourage or develop the trade of the port?

"A. It is quite the contrary. The Great Southern and Western Company's rates for butter coming to Cork are per firkin. The rate from Tralee to Cork, 83 miles on their own line, is 10*d*. per firkin, or 22*s*. 6*d*. per ton; while the rate from Tralee to Liverpool *via* Dublin, a distance of 345 miles, is 30*s*. 10*d*. per ton. From Fermoy to Liverpool *via* Dublin, a distance of 299 miles, the rate

MR. BANKS. is 33s. 4d. per ton. The railway distance is 161 miles, for which the company get about 10s. 10d. per ton, against 15s. 6d. for the 38 miles from Fermoy to Cork. From Kilmallock to Cork, a distance of 41 miles, the rate is 15s. 6d. From Kilmallock to Liverpool, a distance of 262 miles, the rate is 30s. per ton. The Railway Company get about 7s. 11d. for 124 miles, as against 15s. 6d. to Cork, a distance of 41 miles.

"Q. Is this butter the principal article manufactured there by the farmers?

"A. It is. The counties of Limerick and Tipperary, and a great portion of the county of Cork, are almost entirely dependent on the production of butter. I attribute the falling off in the quantity of butter sent to the Cork market to the rates charged by the Great Southern and Western Railway Company.

"Q. Do those arrangements of the Great Southern and Western Railway Company tend in any way to encourage Irish manufactures, as compared with England?

"A. It is quite the contrary. They only get 6s. 6d. out of the Burton beer for 164 miles, while they charge 15s. for 124 miles on the Dublin manufactured beer.

"Q. Is that Guiness' beer?

"A. Guiness', Manders', and others. And for the same article manufactured in Cork, the rate to Faranfore, a distance of 72 miles, is 10s. 10d.; and from Cork to Patrick's Well, a distance of 55 miles, is 11s. 8d.; so that they carry a ton of English ale or porter 165 miles at 6s. 6d., while they charge 11s. 8d. for a ton of the same article manufactured in Cork, over a distance of 55 miles.

"Q. Have you any idea of what difference there is in quantity between English beer which goes to Cork and the Dublin beer?

"A. I should think there is a great deal more of the Dublin beer—ten times as much as the English beer.

"Q. So that the company have not the excuse of having a larger quantity upon which they would make a lower charge?

"A. Nothing of the sort"

MR. ALFRED HICKMAN, examined:—

"Q. You are an ironmaster in South Staffordshire?

"A. I am. I am a manufacturer of pig-iron. I have had acquaintance with the iron trade of

MR. HICKMAN. South Staffordshire for the last thirty years. The pig-iron trade is rapidly becoming defunct.

"Q. To what do you attribute that?

"A. To the excessive railway rates.'

"Q. Can you give some description of the trade during the past and present time, as you know it yourself?

"A. The number of blast furnaces in blast in 1862 was 110, in 1872 there were 102, and now there are only 41.

"Q. Is the trade as at present carried on very profitable?

"A. I have good reason for saying that most of the blast furnaces are carried on either with no profit or some loss.

"Q. Are your blast furnaces well situated with regard to the ironstone fields?

"A. I consider they are very well situated. The thick coal in South Staffordshire is a very fine coal for iron making. I believe pig-iron can be made as cheaply in South Staffordshire as anywhere in the world, if we had fair railway rates.

"Q. Taking the charges upon coal, ironstone, and pig-iron, as you have stated them, have you worked it out to show what the proportion is upon the price of pig-iron?

"A. Yes; the extra price cost on coals above the legal maximum is 3s. 8d. per ton. Then, on ironstone, taking half from Chatterley and half from Frogmore, the excess above the legal maximum is 2s. 4d. on a ton of pig-iron. Then I take the delivery of the iron at 1s. 9d. If you take the figures together, you will find that the total overcharge on a ton of pig-iron amounts to 7s. 9d. per ton above the legal rate. Pig-iron is sold in South Staffordshire at 35s. a ton.

"Q. Upon a fair average quality of pig-iron in South Staffordshire you are paying twenty-five per cent. excessive rates?

"A. Yes.

"Q. Have you ever had occasion to appeal to the Railway Commissioners?

"A. I have often had occasion to do so, but I have never done so, as I have been afraid.

"Q. Why have you been afraid?

"A. Because the Railway Company would hamper my trade, if I came to open rupture with them.

"Q. So the result has been that you have not

MR. HICKMAN. resisted any unjust demand; you have preferred to suffer?

"A. Yes. The Chatterley Iron Company took the North Stafford Railway Company before the Railway Commissioners, and obtained a decision in their favour. Upon this the Railway Company refused to carry for them at all. Then the Chatterley Company went to the commissioners upon that, and the commissioners said that the Railway Company should pay £50 a day while they refused. Being obliged to carry the stuff, they sent the trains at inconvenient times, or allowed the trucks to accumulate; and then the Chatterley Company had to cross the line with a bridge, but the North Stafford Company gave the Chatterley Company notice to take it down. In fact, the Chatterley Company were so hampered with these vexatious proceedings, that they were obliged to compromise the matter.

"Q. The Lincolnshire district compares very favourably with South Staffordshire, so far as rates are concerned?

"A. Yes. Then, taking Warwickshire coal from Haunchwood Colliery to Portsmouth, a distance of 197 miles, the rate is 7s. 10d.; to

Lincoln, a distance of 80 miles, the rate is 4s. 3d.; to Bristol, a distance of 106 miles, the rate is 5s.; to Nottingham, 47 miles, the rate is 3s. 4d.; and to Rugby, 34 miles, the rate is 2s.; but the rate to Wolverhampton from the same colliery, a distance of 30 miles, is 4s. 3d., while, as I have said, to Rugby it is 34 miles for 2s.

Mr. Hickman.

"Q. How do you account for the extraordinary discrepancy?

"A. I can only suppose that when the Midland Company came into Wolverhampton, they came into the combination, or what you were pleased to call 'The Ring.'

"Q. Did not Mr. Allport, the manager of the Midland Company, state on oath before a committee of the House, that if the Midland Company were allowed to come into this district, and to make the line they were proposing, it would result in a very large reduction of the rate?

"A. It was his opinion that it would.

"Q. Is this the evidence to which you refer: 'The London and North-Western Company are the people who have fixed the rates, but they are too high. I have no hesitation in saying that, looking at the iron district in the country, the

MR. HICKMAN.
South Staffordshire rates are too high.' And then the learned counsel asked, 'Do you agree with that opinion? A. I do. Then, again, he was asked, 'It will be a permanent reduction of rates?' And his answer was, 'I should think so.' Is that the evidence Mr. Allport gave?

"A. Precisely.

"Q. And the result of it has been that the rates of the Midland Company, instead of being reduced to the rates they would be able to run at on their own line, have been raised to the level of the rate of the London and North-Western Company?

"A. Practically, they have been.

"Q. As a matter of fact, so far as goods are concerned, you have not derived the slightest advantage?

"A. Not the slightest.

"Q. Therefore, this being so, I presume you would not advise committees of this House to be much influenced by the promises of reduced rates, when made by Railway Companies on asking for new lines?

"A. It will be desirable, I think, to have them in a binding form.

"Q. Have any of the rates been raised lately?

"A. Yes; we had a rise lately upon the North Staffordshire Railway into South Staffordshire, amounting to seven and a half per cent." [Since this evidence was given, I have received notice from the North Staffordshire Railway of a corresponding reduction.]

Mr. Hickman.

"Q. Is it your decided opinion that, unless the companies reduce the rates complained of to about the level of the Northamptonshire rate, the extinction of the Staffordshire iron trade is but a question of time?

"A. It is."

MR. BENJAMIN HINGLEY, examined :—

"Q. You are chairman of the South Staffordshire Ironmasters' Association?

"A. I am. I am the owner of ironworks and collieries, and of ironstone mines at Dudley.

"Q. How many years have you been engaged in the iron trade?

"A. For nearly forty years, and my father before me.

"Q. When you began business, what was the nearest station to your works?

"A. Wednesfield Heath, near Wolverhampton.

Mr. HINGLEY.

"Q. What was the station to station rate in those days, from Wednesfield Heath to Wolverhampton?

"A. It was 7s. 6d., and at one time 6s. 6d.

"Q. What is it now?

"A. It is 11s. from Dudley, and 10s. 6d. from Wolverhampton.

"Q. Had you any facilities for sending your traffic by canal?

"A. Yes; we could send it cheaply and rapidly when required, at least comparatively so. Private carriers also found boats.

"Q. Were there many of those private carriers?

"A. There were many in those days. They competed very considerably, both with the Canal Company and the railway. They brought the rate down to 6s. 6d. at one time.

"Q. Now most of the lines in your district have been amalgamated by two companies, have they not?

"A. Yes.

"Q. Did the Railway Companies buy up the canals?

"A. They have bought up, or in some way arranged to control all the important ones.

"Q. The railway rate has been increased, has it not, since the absorption of the canals?

"A. The railway and canal rate have been both increased.

"Q. The railway raised the canal rate to their own rate?

"A. The rates have all been raised by the action of the Railway Company.

"Q. And upon what ground did the Railway Companies obtain those powers from Parliament, enabling them to absorb the canals?

"A. The grounds publicly stated were, that it would promote economy and enable them to carry at reduced rates.

"Q. How did they support that? Did they say they would be able to work the undertaking more cheaply?

"A. That they would be able to reduce the charges, and promote economy and work more cheaply.

"Q. You have compared your rates, I suppose, with various places where there is sea competition?

"A. From South Wales to London, taking an average distance of 170 miles, the charge for bar-iron is 12s. per ton. From Dudley to London,

MR. HINGLEY.
a distance of 126 miles, the rate is 15s. From Middlesborough to Liverpool, the rate is 9s. 6d.; and from Wolverhampton to Liverpool, which is about half the distance by railway, the charge is 10s. 6d.

"Q. You believe that the effect of Parliament, having allowed the Railway Companies to absorb the canals, has been disastrous to the trade of your district?

"A. It has, indeed.

"Q. Do you think the existence of the finished iron trade is at all endangered?

"A. I think it is imperilled, and may be likely to come to a stop if some alteration is not made.

"Q. Of course, the result would be very disadvantageous to the Railway Company?

"A. I consider it a very short-sighted policy.

"Q. You cannot give me any reason for it?

"A. The reason is, that the companies compete at low rates to places where there is competition, and make us pay the difference, as long as they are able."

MR. THOMAS SWAN, examined:—

"Q. You are a member of the firm of Swan and Sons, Edinburgh?

"A. I am.

"Q. And your business is that of a salesman of stock? How many years have you been established?

"A. About forty-three years.

"Q. What is the rate now on dead meat, from Liverpool to London?

"A. It is 50s. for home meat, and 25s. for American.

"Q. You assume, I suppose, that the rates upon foreign meat and cattle, charged by Railway Companies, are fairly remunerative rates to the Railway Companies?

"A. I presume so.

"Q. Then those charged for home produce are considerably more than remunerative rates?

"A. No doubt."

Mr. Swan.

MR. JOHN SAUNDERS, examined :—

"Q. You are the proprietor of the Cookley Iron Works, at Kidderminster?

"A. Yes; I am a partner in them.

"Q. And the oldest firm in the district?

"A. Yes.

"Q. Now, will you kindly give us the distance

Mr. Saunders.

and the rate from your works at Cookley to London?

"A. The distance is 148 miles, and the rate is 17s. 6d.

"Q. Now, I will ask you to give me the distance from the same districts to Liverpool?

"A. From Llanelly to Liverpool, the distance is 187 miles, and the rate is 12s. 6d. From Swansea to Liverpool, a distance of 192 miles, the rate is 12s. 6d.

"Q. Now, will you give us the rates and distance from Cookley to Southampton?

"A. The distance is 158 miles, and the charge is 21s. 8d.

"Q. Then, as a matter of fact, you are paying 21s. 8d. from Cookley to Southampton, a distance of 158 miles, while Swansea only pays 15s. for 222 miles?

"A. Yes."

Mr. Samuel Skinner, examined:—

"Q. You come from Leeds, near Maidstone?
"A. Yes.
"Q. Can you give the committee some of your experience with regard to hops?

"A. With regard to the carriage of hops to London, on the South-Eastern Railway, I will take Canterbury, which is seventy miles; the rate per ton is 39s. From Dartford, which is seventeen miles, the rate is 22s. 9d. From Eltham, which is nine and a half miles, the charge is 19s. 6d. From Gravesend, which is twenty-four miles, the charge is 26s.; and from Maidstone, which is forty-two and a half miles, the charge is 32s. 6d. per ton.

"Q. Is the dissatisfaction general amongst the hop and fruit growers of Kent and districts?

"A. Yes. To Manchester, upon the Midland, the distance is 190 miles, and the charge is 40s. per ton; and to Liverpool, upon the Midland, the charge is 37s. 6d., and the distance 229 miles.

"Q. I suppose that what you want to deduce is this, that if the company can carry hops from London to Manchester, a distance of 189 miles, for 40s. a ton, it is a gross overcharge to charge 16s. 3d. for ten miles from Beckenham to London?

"A. Just so.

"Q. Again, if they carry hops from London to Liverpool, a distance of 229 miles, at 37s. 6d., it is a gross overcharge to carry from Canterbury to London, a distance of seventy miles, at 39s.?

MR. SKINNER.

"A. That is what we intend to show.

"Q. Will you give the committee the dues by Dieppe?

"A. By Newhaven, delivered into the warehouse in the borough by the Brighton Company, the charge is 17s. per ton; that is a distance of 121 miles.

"Q. And you pay from Beckenham to London, a distance of ten miles, 16s. 3d. per ton?

"A. Yes."

MR. THOMAS ALEXANDER DICKSON, examined:—

"Q. You were formerly a member of the House of Commons?

"A. I was.

"Q. You are now a member of the Royal Commission for inquiring into inland navigation in Ireland, and you are also a member of the Chamber of Commerce at Belfast?

"A. I am.

"Q. You have no competition with railways in Ireland?

"A. We have not.

"Q. Do you consider the present tariff in rates is such as to develop the industry of the country?

"A. I consider that in the great majority of cases the rates are prohibitory, especially in connection with agricultural produce and local manufactures. Take pork, which is an article largely consumed in Ireland. The rate charged for about forty miles of railway carriage from Dungannon to Belfast is 13s. 4d. a ton, not carted at either end; adding 2s. 6d. for cartage, it would bring it up to 15s. 10d. On the other hand, the rate charged for American bacon coming the same distance, from Belfast into the interior for forty miles, is only 10s., including cartage at each end, giving 5s. 10d. per ton against the Irish producer.

"Q. With regard to the charges on flax, are they higher per mile for the Irish flax than for the foreign flax?

"A. Yes. The rate from Stranorlan, a town in County Donegal, is, for flax, 21s. 8d., to Belfast, a distance of eighty-six miles; while the rate from Cohent, in Belgium, is only 18s. 8d. *Taking distance in Donegal, you can convey bread stuffs from America to Londonderry at about one-half the rate that you can from Londonderry into the interior of County Donegal.* It takes more to convey produce from Donegal to its market in

MR. DICKSON. Londonderry than it does from America to Londonderry. From Dublin to Tenderagee, a distance of eighty-two miles, the rate is 15s. per ton; whereas from Dublin to Portadown, a distance of eighty-seven miles, a station beyond Tenderagee, the rate is 9s. 2d. per ton. From Consett, near Newcastle-on-Tyne, to Belfast via Ardrossan, a distance of 260 miles, the rate is 14s. 6d. From Belfast to Enniskillen, a distance of eighty-seven miles, the rate is 14s. 2d. per ton.

"Q. Do you find that these rates have the effect of checking the trade in Ireland?

"A. Undoubtedly so."

MR. FREDERICK BRITTAIN.

"Q. Are you president of the Sheffield Chamber of Commerce?

"A. I am. The trade has diminished very largely the last few years. Until about 1872, the steel nail trade increased rapidly, and the works were pretty well employed till about 1875.

"Q. Have you made a computation of the falling off in steel nails this year?

"A. Mr. George Wilson, of the firm of Cammell and Co., states he believes if the depression continues, there will be a falling off of 100,000 tons this year, as compared to last. Mr. Wilson is accidentally prevented from coming before the Chamber.

Mr. Brittain.

"Q. Is the decline in trade in any way attributable to railway rates?

"A. To a considerable extent. The rate from Sheffield to Hull is 1·7*d.* per ton per mile; the rate from Middlesborough is 0·95*d.* per ton per mile. The rate from Sheffield to Goole is 2·72*d.*, and from Middlesborough to Goole 1·15*d.* From Sheffield to Liverpool, the rate is 1·4*d.*; and from Middlesborough to Liverpool, 0·9*d.* per mile. The steel nails sent from Sheffield to Hull, Goole, Liverpool, and London, pay on an average 1·73*d.* per ton per mile; while the nails from Middlesborough to the same ports pay 0·73*d.* per ton per mile; that is to say, Sheffield pays twice as much as Liverpool.

"Q. Have you any other mode of conveyance to the sea?

"A. There was a canal years ago; but now we have not the competition of the canal, because it is the property of the Railway Company. I think it is exceedingly probable that the high rates of

MR. BRITTAIN.
carriage to the ports have had something to do with the loss to the English trade in steel nails; because in 1870 our export of railway iron amounted to more than a million tons; in 1879 it amounted to 463,000 tons, which shows a falling off to half; *whereas in the same time many of our competing nations increased very rapidly indeed.*

"Q. Then the effects of these high rates have been really disastrous to trade?

"A. It has. During the last few years the population of the iron districts has fallen off very much indeed. We have had rows of houses empty; and the value of property has fallen immensely. In 1871, we had 2500 empty houses; this year we have 5200."

THE HON. FREDERICK STRUTT.

"Q. Are you a partner with your brother, Lord Belper, in some cotton mills at Belper; and are you the president of the Chamber of Commerce at Derby?

"A. Yes.

"Q. You contend, I believe, or the Chamber of Commerce contends, that advantages are given to other towns by the Railway Companies at lower rates than to Derby?

"A. Yes.

"Q. The Burton brewer can send his ale to Derby at a less cost than the Derby brewer can produce it on the spot, cannot he?

"A. Yes. I shall prove that on account of the advantages the Burton brewers have with regard to the carriage of the materials from which beer is made.

"Q. And you contend that this undue preference affects to the same extent the malting trade, which is carried on extensively at Derby?

"A. It is carried on extensively, and, I believe, it would be more so with different rates. From Derby to Penrith, a distance of 165 miles, the rate per ton is 27s. 6d.; from Burton to Penrith, a distance of 177 miles, the rate is 15s. 2d., making an excess to the disadvantage of Derby of 9s. 4d. per ton. This would amount to 2s. per barrel, and is irrespective of the rebate for loading and unloading the various articles used in the manufacture of ale, which no doubt the Burton brewers enjoy. I have no actual evidence before me, because it is impossible to get at the agreements between

HON. F. STRUTT.

large firms, as at Burton, and the Railway Companies.

"Q. It is enough if you say that in your knowledge rebates are given.

"A. I know that rebates are given.

"Q. Now, will you take carriage of hops from London to Derby?

"A. The distance from London to Derby is 129 miles, and the rate charged for the carriage is 35s. per ton carted. From London to Burton the distance is 122 miles, and the rate is 21s. 8d., station to station, and if you add cartage, 6s. 6d., from London, that would make 28s. 2d.; this would show an excess to the disadvantage of Derby of 6s. 10d. per ton.

"Q. The rebate would be plus that, would it not?

"A. The allowance would be in addition to the difference.

"Q. Now, will you take the case of grain from Cambridge to Derby?

"A. The distance is 105 miles, and 13s. 4d. is the actual rate. From Cambridge to Burton the charge is 10s. 7d., a distance of 103 miles, and the computed weight, which would be six quarters per ton—that is to say, in the Derby case—is carried at the actual weight of five quarters per ton, and to Burton at the computed weight of six quarters per ton. That is one of the arrangements. It is not exactly in the form of a rebate, and I am, perhaps, not prepared to give you actual evidence of the fact; but it is notorious to every trader in Derby that it is so.

"Q. "Therefore, the result would be, that it costs Derby, how much per quarter?

"A. It costs Derby 2s. 8d. per quarter, and Burton 1s. 9¼d. per quarter. Of course, I need not point out that in these days of narrow profits that represents a profit. From Lancaster to Derby, a distance of 137 miles, the rate is 15s. 10d. per ton; and from Lancaster to Burton, a distance of 149 miles, that is twelve miles further, the charge is 11s. 9d., computed weight to Burton and actual weight to Derby.

"Q. That is a worse case, is it not?

"A. It is, perhaps, rather a worse case; because the distance is in favour of Derby.

"Q. What is the result of these charges?

"A. We believe that it has made it almost impossible to compete with Burton. To show what

HON. F. STRUTT. a gross anomaly it is, I may say that it is no infrequent thing for firms carrying on their business at Derby to send their grain from the town where they have bought it to Burton, where the company have to unload, warehouse it, enter it in its books, advise the owner of it, reload it into trucks, and carry it to Derby reconsigned. This custom enables the Derby trader to save some amount in cost of transit over the cost, if he had it sent to Derby in the first place."

MR. WILLIAM FLETCHER.

" Q. You reside at Brigham Hill, Carlisle, do you not?

" A. I do.

" Q. You wish to give evidence on behalf of the West Cumberland Coal Association?

" A. I do.

" Q. Are you a Justice of the Peace for Cumberland, and until lately member of Parliament for Cockermouth?

" A. Yes.

" Q. Did not the Maryport and Carlisle Railway Company convert their debenture capital into ordinary stock?

" A. Yes.

"Q. To disguise the dividend?

"A. Yes, that was the case. The Maryport and Carlisle Railway Company for ten or twelve years have been dividing upon the average from ten to twelve per cent. per annum. The coal-owners, who were losing money, partly in consequence of the high rates, thought it a fit time to apply to the company for some reduction of those rates. The application was not granted; but immediately afterwards the company took the extraordinary, and, I fancy, unprecedented course, in order, as we suppose, to conceal the real magnitude of their profits, of converting nearly the whole of their preference and debenture capital into ordinary stock, and that ordinary stock was allotted to the existing shareholders at par, whilst it was worth, in the market, a premium of at least one hundred and twenty per cent. Notwithstanding that extraordinary financial performance, the dividends have since been maintained at very much the same point as before. The dividend for the last half year was ten per cent.

"Q. Do you complain, as colliery owners, of any undue preference being given?

"A. Yes; we complain that the rates are

Mr. Fletcher.

excessive, inasmuch as they are higher than the rates charged in other colliery districts with which we have to compete in Ireland. I may explain that the bulk of the coal raised in West Cumberland is exported to Ireland; and there we came into competition with coal from South Wales, Lancashire and the West of Scotland. The coal rates in all these districts being very considerably less—in some cases they are only one-half, and in other cases thirty per cent. less than ours—we are, to use the expression I used before, handicapped in the coal trade, in consequence of our rates being higher than the rates of competing districts. And we not only complain of their being too high on the ground of fairness and reasonableness, but we complain that the companies, especially the Maryport and Carlisle Company, give a preference to distant freighters over the local coal-owners. I have here one or two examples. To save the time of the committee, I have only brought one or two, but I may say they are fairly representative. The coal rate from Brayton to Maryport, a distance of nine miles, in the company's waggons is 1s. 5d. per ton for shipment, and 1s. 11d. for land sale; but from Carlisle to Maryport, a distance of twenty-eight miles, over three times as far, the company brings coal from Scotland and Newcastle at 1s. 8½d. per ton in owner's waggons, which is equal to 2s. per ton in company's waggons for shipment, and 1s. 11d. per ton in owner's waggons (equal to 2s. 2¼d. in company's waggons) for land sale."

MR. FLETCHER.

MR. JAMES DUNCAN.

"Q. You are a sugar refiner, carrying on business in London, are you not?

"A. I am.

"Q. And you are here to represent not only yourself, but the sugar refiners and dealers in London?

"A. I am.

"Q. What do you complain of in respect of the railway rates?

"A. We have to complain of the preferential rates in favour of Greenock chiefly, and also in favour of the Continent.

"Q. Have you taken out the rates for a number of towns, from Greenock to London, and ascertained what are the rates charged per mile upon sugar by the Railway Companies to those different towns?

MR. DUNCAN.

"A. Yes, I have. I have taken the rates of thirty-nine towns from London and from Greenock.

"Q. What is the general result that comes out from a comparison of the figures charged from Greenock to those thirty-nine towns, and from London to the thirty-nine towns? What bounty do you say is offered to Greenock?

"A. A ton of sugar from the Clyde is carried 292 miles for 26s. 6½d., and from London a ton of sugar is carried 150 miles for 26s. 7½d., or roughly, sugar from Greenock is brought 300 miles for the same rate that London sugar is carried 150 miles, the station to station mileage rate from London being double that from the Clyde.

"Q. And assuming that you get your London sugar carried at the same rate as it is from Greenock, how much lower would that be?

"A. We ought to get it, instead of paying 26s. 7½d., at 13s. 7½d.

"Q. So it comes to this, that there is a higher charge upon you as compared with Greenock of 13s., or, to put it otherwise, the Greenock refiners have a bounty of 13s. at your cost?

"A. This is so.

"Q. What alterations do you recommend?

"A. There was a memorial prepared by the London Sugar Trade Association, and perhaps the committee will allow me to read from it."

Mr. Duncan.

The memorial was read as follows :—

"'The memorial of the undersigned respectfully showeth—1. That they are appointed by the sugar refiners and wholesale grocers of London, representing about one-third of the sugar trade of the United Kingdom, for the purpose of attending to the interests of the trade in connection with railway rates and charges.

"' 2. That their trade is seriously injured by the practice of Railway Companies of charging unequal rates for the conveyance of the same and similar goods, as between different towns ; the rates charged for sugar sent from London being very much higher in proportion than the rates charged for sugar sent from rival trading districts in this country, and for foreign sugar.

"'This preference is, in effect, a bounty to rival manufacturers and traders, and diverts the course of trade from its natural channel.

"'By these unequal charges, the London sugar trade is seriously injured.

"' 3. That to prevent the disastrous results of the

Mr. Duncan. preference given by Railway Companies to certain towns and foreign countries upon the general trade of the country, the law as to illegal preference should be more clearly defined and enforced; and your memorialists would suggest that each Railway Company should be compelled to carry the same or similar goods on its own system at a uniform rate, except where the sanction of the Railway Commissioners has been first obtained, and where an inequality was justified by difference in the actual cost of conveyance.

"'4. That the powers of the Railway Commissioners should be continued and enlarged, and that they should have power to *stop* illegal charges.'"

Evidence continued :—

"Q. Do you think that any body less powerful than the State is competent to keep the Railway Companies within their privileges under their Acts of Parliament?

"A. I do not.

"Q. And that that duty ought to be undertaken by the State, which has given them these special privileges?

"A. Certainly."

I shall come presently to the evidence given by Mr. Grotrian, and with reference to it, I must refer my readers to the remarks made in my opening chapter, respecting the claim which railway directors make to be allowed to compete in a race in which they not only decide the weights to be carried by themselves, but also those to be borne by their competitors.

I will now give an instance of how these weights are apportioned. Mr. Pease, the member for South Durham, was a member of the Select Committee, and is a very extensive coal-owner in Durham. He is, in addition, a director of the North-Eastern Railway, and, if we may judge from his cross-examination of witnesses, a firm believer in the preferential system. Now, there are two coal fields in the north-eastern portion of England —one situated in the Northumberland and Durham district, and the other in South and West Yorkshire, and both are very extensive. The ports on which the former district principally depend for the shipment of coal are Newcastle and Hartlepool, whilst for the latter district Hull is the chief port. The North-Eastern Company possess the only railway which gives access to these ports. The coal-owners of South and West Yorkshire have, therefore, to go to the North-Eastern Board, of which Mr. Pease is a member, to find out on what terms they may be allowed to compete with Mr. Pease and his brother coal-owners in all foreign markets for which Hull is the shipping port. In order to show what these terms are, I will now refer to the evidence of Mr. Massey on the subject.

Mr. W. A. Massey.

"Q. You are a partner in the firm of Massey and Sawyer, steamship owners and coal exporters; and you are also a member of the Hull Corporation, and a member of the Hull Chamber of Commerce?

"A. I am.

"Q. Can you give the committee any information with regard to the rates for the conveyance of coal?

"A. Yes; I will endeavour to do so. In the course of my travels, selling coal as a coal merchant, I have found the North-Eastern Railway Company invariably foster their trade in the North by giving cheap rates to the northern coal-owners; and I will give two or three instances of the fact, briefly.

"Q. Will you state to the committee the rates from South and West Yorkshire collieries to Hull?

"A. From Monk Breton Colliery to Hull, a distance of fifty-eight miles, the rate is 3s. 1d.; that works out to a rate per ton per mile of 0·638d., exclusive of waggon hire. From the Denaby Main to Hull, forty-seven miles, the rate is 2s. 10d., or 0·723d., per ton per mile. That colliery is in South Yorkshire, and they do a large business with Hull. We have found, as importers, that the collieries in the North compete very strongly with us, by reason of the cheap rates which they have given them. For instance, the Radcliff Colliery, in Northumberland, to the Tyne Dock, a distance of forty-three miles, has a rate of 1s. 6¾d., or 0·436d., per ton per mile. The Ashington Colliery, to the Tyne, a distance of thirty miles, has a rate of 11⅞d., or 0·396d., per ton per mile. Broomhill Colliery to the Tyne, a distance of forty-two miles, has a rate of 1s. 6½d., or 0·440d., per ton per mile.

"Q. Are those rates in favour of the northern ports?

"A. Yes, they are. The highest rate we have is Denaby Main, which is 0·723d. to Hull, against the charge from Ashington to Newcastle of 0·396d.

"Q. Are you aware whether other Railway

Companies adopt the same system, whenever they are the owners of docks on their lines?

"A. I cannot speak positively on that point."

In addition, however, to this, it is, of course, of great moment to both of these districts that ships bringing goods into the country should come to their respective ports, because these ships usually take coal as a return cargo. Hull, being considerably nearer the great centres of trade, has necessarily an advantage in this respect; but, as will be seen by Mr. Grotrian's evidence, that advantage has been confiscated by the North-Eastern Company, by the simple expedient of giving Newcastle and Hartlepool practically the same rate for goods as Hull.

Then, again, both districts compete in London, Yorkshire having, of course, the great natural advantages of proximity. Now, the North-Eastern Company cannot be regarded as a cheap line, if one can believe Mr. Rowlandson's evidence, or that of Mr. Grotrian. The latter gentleman states as a fact, that the tonnage rate per mile from Hull is higher than that of any other railways to or from any port in the kingdom. But it happens, curiously enough, that it alternates from being the dearest line in the kingdom to the cheapest; for the evidence showed that for the carriage of coal from Mr. Pease's district to London, to compete with Yorkshire coal, the company only charge at the rate of 0·39*d*. per ton per mile, which is a less rate than is charged for carriage of coal in any other part of the United Kingdom. Now, Mr. Pease's board justify all this on the plea that the public reap the advantage through increased competition, and, for the sake of argument, I will for the moment admit the hypothesis. How comes it, however, that this artificially competitive arrangement is only allowed to exercise its beneficent influence in one direction, and that direction being invariably away from and not towards Mr. Pease's district? Let us see what Mr. Grotrian has to say on the subject.

Mr. Frederick Brent Grotrian.

"Q. Are you a merchant residing in Hull?

"A. I am.

"Q. And one of the commissioners of the Humber Conservancy?

"A. Yes.

MR. GRO-TRIAN.

"Q. And you are also a justice of the peace?

"A. I am.

"Q. Has the result of the North-Eastern Company's system been to divert the trade from Hull to the northern ports?

"A. Yes, doubtless. I may perhaps give some illustration of the rates which exist. I have a statement here of the rates charged for the carriage of timber and deal from Hull to Leeds. From Hull to Leeds, a distance of fifty-one miles, the rate is 7s. 11d.; and from West Hartlepool to Leeds, a distance of seventy-two miles, that is, from the Docks of West Hartlepool, which are owned by the North-Eastern Railway Company, it is the same rate, namely, 7s. 11d. From Newcastle Tyne Dock, also owned by the North-Eastern Company, to Leeds, a distance of ninety-three miles, the rate is also 7s. 11d.; so that, as a matter of fact, the rates are the same, although the distance is very much longer.

"Q. Can you give one other illustration to the committee?

"A. I can give hundreds, if it is necessary.

"Q. Will you give the rate from Hull to Barnsley, if you have it?

"A. From Hull to Barnsley, a distance of 61 miles, the rate is 9s. 2d.

"Q. Is that for timber and deals?

"A. Yes. From West Hartlepool, from the North-Eastern Railway Company's Docks, the rate is 9s. 2d., the distance being 96 miles, and from Newcastle-on-Tyne to Barnsley, a distance of 116 miles, the charge is 10s.

"Q. So that they are very nearly the same rates, notwithstanding that the distance is nearly double from the Tyne to Barnsley, as compared with that from Hull to Barnsley?

"A. Yes. If you will allow me, I will give another illustration. To Manchester from Hull, a distance of 91 miles, the charge is 15s. From West Hartlepool to Manchester, a distance of 114 miles, the rate is also 15s., and from Newcastle, a distance of 136 miles, the rate is also 15s. I have given those places as typical places, but really and truly they embrace hundreds of other places. For instance, Manchester would embrace a group of places, and the same with Sheffield.

"Q. Do you find that this system of favouring the northern ports tends to divert the trade from Hull?

MR. GRO-
TRIAN.

"A. I have no doubt of it. I should like to give another illustration. Take Pontefract, the distance from Hull being 42 miles, the rate is 7s. 6d. From West Hartlepool, a distance of 81 miles, the rate is 8s. 4d. From Newcastle, a distance of 101 miles, the rate is also 8s. 4d. Now, there is a difference there in distance of 59 miles. It is 59 miles longer from Pontefract to Newcastle than from Hull, while the only addition to the rate is 10d. Now, I want to take another case, to show how the system is applied with regard to Hull. Take Brancepeth, which is 106 miles from Hull, and the charge is 14s. 7d. It is 5s. 10d. for 30 miles from West Hartlepool, and 5s. for 21 miles from Newcastle. Now, there is a difference there of 76 miles as against Hull. *When we want to go north, and the distance there is against us, there is an addition of 8s. 9d. for 76 miles; but when the northern ports (Newcastle, for example) want to come south, they carry 59 miles further for* 10d. *extra.*

"Q. Does the North-Eastern Company adopt the same principle invariably?

"A. They adopt one principle, I think, invariably, and that is this—that wherever there is traffic to come south to that district, which belongs as it were geographically to Hull, they carry, as I have attempted to show, any distance at the same rate; that is to say, when the company has to bring it down south from their own docks, to compete with Hull, or the docks at Hull. Now, the system they adopt, on the other hand, from Hull, is invariably a mileage rate, when we want to go into a district which is served by the Tyne and Hartlepool, so that, as a matter of fact, the effect of it is this— *that all places near the Tyne and Hartlepool, which belong geographically to those places, are reserved exclusively to them by the action of the North-Eastern Railway Company; whereas all the places to which we have the advantage, geographically, of access and position, are also opened out on equal terms to the northern ports."*

Mr. Grotrian.

So that it comes to this, that a principle which is beneficial in its operation when applied to Durham and the south, is simply out of the question in respect to Yorkshire and the north. Now, in these remarks, there is not the slightest intention of saying anything personally disrespectful of Mr. Pease. He is simply the embodiment of a system, the advantage and necessity of which he has for so many years heard dinned into the ears of committees and the public generally, by railway authorities, and in which he now probably most thoroughly believes. But whatever may be the opinion of this gentleman, I think it must be clear to any unprejudiced mind that for a trader or body of traders to be allowed to inaugurate such a system as I have described—affecting, as it does to so large an extent, the varied interests of competitors and persons scattered over hundreds of miles of country, and to do all this at their own sweet will and pleasure—is, to say the least of it, one of the most striking and at the same time pernicious anomalies ever recorded in the annals of a commercial country; and my opinion in that respect is not in the least shaken by the fact that the Select Committee arrived at a distinctly opposite conclusion.

Mr. Peter Spence.

"Q. You are the proprietor of chemical works at Manchester, are you not?

"A. I am.

"Q. And you are interested largely in chemical works also at Birmingham, Bradford, and Goole?

"A. I am.

"Q. And I believe you produce about the largest quantity of one chemical article, alum, of any manufacturer in the world?

MR. SPENCE.

"A. Yes; I suppose I am the largest maker of alum.

"Q. You turn out about 10,000 tons of that annually, do you not?

"A. Yes.

"Q. And the views which you have upon this question of railway rates you have embodied in a memorandum, as I understand. Will you now proceed to make your statement?

"A. I will. I have brought it under different headings. The first is 'Excessive rates for alum, copperas, and other chemicals, between Manchester and Liverpool.' The rate for alum and copperas from Manchester to Liverpool, a distance of 31½ miles, is 7s. 6d. per ton; but if proportioned to the rate from Manchester to London, which is 186 miles for 18s. 4d., it would be 3s. 1d.; if proportioned to the rate from Manchester to Bristol, which is 178 miles for 15s., it would be 2s. 8d.; if to the rate from Manchester to Glasgow, which is 225¼ miles for 15s., it would be 2s. 1d.

"Though I am almost daily corresponding all

I

MR. SPENCE.

over the country for rates, I do not know a single case where the railway monopoly is not complete and where there are two Railway Companies offering competitive rates. I now beg to cite an illustration afforded by the Manchester and Liverpool case. Although the men of Manchester and Liverpool were the first to construct a great railway, I speak advisedly when I say that so far as goods transit between these cities is concerned, the invention of the locomotive has proved to be an unmixed evil. The charges per ton per mile of the four Railway Companies who are battening upon this traffic, are nearly four times those between Manchester and Glasgow; and the South Lancashire trader is in this way annually fleeced of hundreds of thousands of pounds.

"The following figures show that a waggon and horses road-service could carry the goods for twenty-five per cent. less than the present charges of the companies. On the nearly level road between Manchester and Liverpool, a man, two horses, and a waggon, could in three days take four tons of goods from Manchester to Liverpool, and bring four tons back, at a cost of 15s. per day, or 45s. in all. As the station to station rate of the companies is 7s. 6d. per ton, their charge for carrying four tons to Liverpool and bringing four tons back is 60s. A plate railway has recently been proposed, which would admit the use of the ordinary road waggon wheels, and thus save all terminal expenses at stations. By a ship canal betwixt Manchester and Liverpool, the economy of carriage would obviously be far greater than by any other system, steam navigation being, beyond controversy, the cheapest known mode of inland transit. I may add that the Manchester ship canal scheme has the approval of able engineers. All three modes of relief are, however, practically denied to the South Lancashire manufacturer. If a Bill were promoted in Parliament for a horse tramway or ship canal, either proposal would meet with the determined opposition of four powerful Railway Companies; and if any of these schemes were actually inaugurated, it would have to face a long struggle with the companies, who would reduce their rates in the hope of starving it into the 'conference,' and the consequent acceptance of their former oppressive tariff.

"This actually took place under the spurt of competition twenty years ago, when the rate was

MR. SPENCE.

Mr. Spence.

reduced to 2s. 6d. per ton. Now, since Parliament has interfered with the laws of supply and demand to the extent of protecting these four companies against unlimited competition by other railway promoters, I submit that the Lancashire manufacturer has a right to demand that it shall require them to make reasonable rates, and also to abstain from using their enormous capital to crush any attempt he may make to provide a radically cheaper mode of carriage. On this branch of the subject, I would say that if the result of this committee's labours is to fix the railway rates of the country, and to prevent them being lowered, merely for the sake of destroying water-carriage competition, there is no doubt that the scheme of a Manchester ship canal will be undertaken at once, and I for one will be happy to take shares in it.

"I may illustrate the railway mode of facilitating through traffic on canals by stating my experience in connection with a recent inquiry. A few weeks ago, my representative, having called on the agent of the Manchester, Sheffield, and Lincolnshire Railway Company to ascertain the through rates of dues for alum to Birmingham, was informed that they could not quote them, except for their own canal, as the other canal-owners would object to supply them with the information, and that my only course was to write to each of the three other companies. On writing to these, I found that two of them quoted not a rate per ton, but per 2400 lbs. As the Manchester to Birmingham canal competition has been dealt with in this fashion, it will be readily understood that the Manchester to London traffic has even fared worse. Formerly there was an excellent canal goods service betwixt the two places, the through journey being done in three days and nights. There is now not even the pretence of any through traffic by this route. Last year I made strenuous effort to get a boat-load of goods through from Manchester as far as Aylesbury to a customer there, but I found that, owing to high dues, it would cost me 16s. 8d. per ton by water against 13s. 4d. by rail. The facts regarding the obstructive and oppressive policy of the Birmingham Canal navigations, controlled by the London and North-Western Company, are notorious in the black country, and I need only give one example of its charges for toll. From the Stourbridge Canal to Birmingham, a distance of ten miles over this company's navigation, Stourbridge bricks pay

MR. SPENCE,

MR. SPENCE.

2s. 0½d. per ton, or four-tenths of a mile for a penny. The same goods from Birmingham to London, a distance of 150 miles, over four independent canals, pay 2s. 1½d. per ton, or nearly six miles for a penny. The following figures show how effectively the Great Western Railway Company has strangled the traffic on three of the most important canals it has competed with and ultimately frightened into its embrace. In 1848, the gross traffic and receipts on the Hereford and Gloucester Canal were £5167. In the three successive decades, they had steadily dwindled down till they were only thirty per cent. of this amount. During the same period, the £13,273 of receipts on the Stratford-on-Avon Canal had fallen off till only twenty-three per cent. remained; and within the same thirty years, the £33,741 of receipts on the Kennet and Avon Canal had all been shunted on to the rails, except £4488, or thirteen per cent. The Hereford and Gloucester Canal it is now proposed to kill outright, by converting it into a railway.

"I will now deal with the general policy of the Railway Companies with regard to canals. The whole policy of the companies owning or leasing canals is to discourage their use in every possible way, in order to drive the traffic on to their metals. The results in the crowding of their lines with slow heavy goods, thus impeding and endangering their passenger traffic, and glutting their depôts, are in themselves sufficiently serious. But the injury to the manufacturing and trading interests of the country in preventing them availing themselves to the utmost of the advantages of inland water communication, it would be difficult to over-estimate. In France, Holland, and America, the importance of canals is fully recognized, and new ones are frequently being constructed. The canal makes its own station opposite every factory, thus involving no terminal expenses; and the simple fact that the Railway Companies have purchased or otherwise taken under their control fifty-three of the canals of the United Kingdom, most of them so situated as to enable them effectually to control the through traffic, is a clear proof that they did not consider themselves able to compete upon equal terms with horse-towing on the canals. I may, perhaps, be allowed to give instances known to me of violation by Railway Companies of section 17 of the Act of 1873.

Mr. Spence.

MR. SPENCE. Railway Companies have, in the following instances, in districts with which I am connected as a manufacturer, violated the provision in the Act of 1873, requiring them to keep the canals in thorough working condition. The Bolton and Bury Canal, held by the Lancashire and Yorkshire Railway Company, and running parallel with that company's line through the manufacturing district lying between these towns and Manchester, has been allowed by the company to get into a very bad condition. It is unsafe to navigate it at night, and it is, therefore, closed nightly all the year round. When a casualty occurs, nothing like the effort is made to keep the navigation open which would be put forth by the company if their own line were blocked, but matters are allowed to drift, and the repair is undertaken in the most leisurely fashion. The canal, in consequence of a complete breakdown, is stopped at the present moment, and has been so for the last six or eight months; and were it not for the urgent representations of manufacturers on its banks, I doubt very much whether the repairs now in progress would have been undertaken at all. The canal has been allowed by the company to be undermined at one point by a neighbouring colliery.

They had powers to prevent this, but declined to avail themselves of them. A friend of mine, who is a partner in one of the largest chemical works in Lancashire, informs me that the present stoppage is costing his firm over £19 per week, in the additional carriage of one of his materials alone, and that in fact a permanent stoppage of the canal would mean a final closing of his works. By a provision in the Act of Transfer, the company were bound to prevent the silting up of the channel connecting the canal with the River Mersey, but this requirement has been practically ignored; a sand bar has been allowed to accumulate at the entrance to the canal, and, in consequence, there is no exit for loaded vessels during neap tides, that is, during a fortnight of every month. The canals and navigations under the control of the North-Eastern Railway Company have been allowed to go lamentably out of repair. Both the condition of the locks and the want of dredging have rendered them almost impassable, and then at such limited draughts as would be unprofitable to work over, even were the dues not maintained at, I believe, the very maximum allowed by their Acts. In the case of the Market Weighton Canal, it is a fact

MR. SPENCE.

that they exactly doubled them almost immediately after taking possession. In the case of the Huddersfield Canal, the London and North-Western Railway Company maintain the maximum rate of dues allowed by their Act.

"Now, in my opinion, there is no prospect of a remedy, unless the Government takes over the canals. As the gloomy anticipations of the committee of 1872, with regard to the pernicious influence of the Railway Companies over the canals, have been fully borne out by the experience of the last nine years; as the Railway Companies have, both in letter and spirit, violated the provisions of the Act of 1873, requiring them to maintain in perfect condition the canals they possessed before the passage of the Act, and in no way to control or interfere with the traffic upon other canals, but to afford it every reasonable facility in their power; and as, under the existing *régime*, there is no prospect of free and unfettered water carriage competition in many of the most important districts of the country;—it is clear to me that we have now reached the condition of things referred to by a well-known railway authority, Sir Edward Watkin, when, in giving evidence before the Railway Companies' Amalgamation Committee of 1872, he said, at page 452, 'If it can be proved that the advantage of a navigation which Parliament has given to the public has been taken away, I think it would be quite reasonable, on people coming to amalgamate, to say, "You shall give up possession of this thing, which is not properly used."'

"I consider the time has now arrived for Parliament to say once for all to the Railway Companies, 'hands off' the canals. As long as their clear motive is to destroy them, no amount of legislation will prevent them carrying out their object, while they have any power left to do so. England cannot, in the face of increasing foreign competition, afford to see her cheapest means of internal transit year after year closed against traffic; and as all other methods of preserving the canals have failed, I would recommend their being at once taken over by the Government, on the basis of their present actual receipts from tolls, less working expenses, and less the cost of restoring them to the prime working condition prescribed by the Act of 1873. There are other reasons why Government should take over the canals; one very good

MR. SPENCE.

reason is, that many districts of the country are now periodically flooded, to the serious loss of agriculturists and others. The navigation in not a few of these districts, as, for example, betwixt Birmingham and the Humber, suffers so seriously for want of water, that Birmingham has practically no water communication with the Humber ports. If the canals were in the hands of the Government, it would, I presume, have powers to enable it to construct reservoirs at suitable points, which would tend both to prevent the floods and keep the navigations liberally supplied. If, after the Government had obtained possession of the canals, the canal carriers should agree to offer it such an increased toll as would justify the outlay required to adapt them for steam navigation (which is, I think, a very probable event), its centralized administration would enable it to carry out the change with ease. At present, if any single Canal Company did anything in this direction, its expenditure would be worse than thrown away. The short boats of other canals passing through its lengthened locks would waste an enormous amount of water, and the long boats of the improved navigation could not enter the short locks of the unimproved canals. Now, on the question of the suitability of Government for canal administration, although I have naturally a strong repugnance to centralization, I think canal management would be a function for which Government officers are particularly adapted. It would not involve a tithe of the harassment now attending the working of the Postal Letters and Telegraphs Department. Certainly any difficulties of this kind are not to be named in comparison with the gain to the manufacturing and trading interests of the country, by rescuing its waterways from impending destruction by the Railway Companies, or from controlling railway interest in their shares, thus enabling them for the first time to offer a genuine and permanent competition with railway charges over the principal lines of goods traffic."

The above extracts will hardly give my readers more than a faint idea of the complaints from all parts of the kingdom with which the committee was deluged. I have already stated that its work lasted into two sessions; and I say it advisedly, that if evidence had been asked for generally, and the public had dared to make their grievances known, the work of the committee would not yet have been finished.

Professor Hunter gives some remarkable evidence upon this point. He is asked—

<small>PROF. HUNTER.</small> "Q. Have you found individuals unwilling to give evidence against Railway Companies, before this committee, for example?

"A. Yes; in several cases the information I have given has been received upon the express condition that I should not mention the names of people from whom I received it, those being persons of very good position, which surprised me very much.

"Q. Are those individuals apprehensive that they will suffer at the hands of the Railway Companies?

"A. Yes. What people fear about Railway Companies is this—that in ways quite within their legal power they will deliberately use their power to inflict injury by way of retaliation, if the customer objects to anything which they consider illegal.

"Q. Can you give the committee any example of a case which justifies that fear?

"A. I could not give a better example than

a case which was brought before the Railway Commissioners. The plaintiffs were Messrs. J. and F. Howard, one of the members of that firm being a member of this House, and the defendants being a most respectable Railway Company, the Midland Railway Company. The Messrs. Howard disputed the charges of the Railway Company in respect to terminals, and, as it ultimately turned out, they were not right in their contentions, but they threatened to take proceedings before the Railway Commissioners. The Midland Company retaliated by raising their rates to Bedford more than 100 per cent., and not to other parts of the line—in fact, to such an extent, that if they had succeeded, it would have amounted to a fine of £1500 or £2000 a year upon Messrs. Howard. That practice continued up to the second day of the hearing ; and, in support of my statement, I may quote what was stated by the Commissioners in their judgment, which is dated the 1st of June, 1878 : 'These changes,' that is to say, the increasing of the rates, 'applied to no place but Bedford, and establishing as they did preferential rates between other places on the lines of the two companies and Bedford, and doing this for no other

(margin: Prof. Hunter.)

PROF. HUNTER. purpose but to retaliate upon Messrs. Howard for claiming a terminal allowance, were a distinct abuse of the powers entrusted to Railway Companies of regulating their charges of conveyance; an abuse, indeed, that was so plain that, on the second day of the hearing, the counsel for the companies informed us that, foreseeing that we should have no alternative but to set aside such rates, he would not say a word in defence of them, and that the two companies, advised by him, had resolved to cancel them forthwith, and to readjust all accounts from November upon the footing of the rates which had been in force up to then, and which would at once be reverted to.'"

RAILWAY EVIDENCE.

THE evidence on behalf of the Railway Companies, as I have previously remarked, was of a most exhaustive character, so much so that at times it had a tendency to become somewhat garrulous. The prevalent idea seemed to be, that any difficulty was best dealt with by generalizing, and this mode of procedure produced a somewhat confusing effect.

The defence did not so much rely on a denial of the charges made by the public as far as figures were concerned in the relation to maximum and preferential rates, as to an elaborate defence of the principle on which these rates were made. With regard to the maximum rates, the extracts from the evidence will give a pretty accurate idea of the railway opinions on the subject, and will also to some extent explain their views on the preferential system. But with regard to the question of preference, the Permanent Secretary of the Board of Trade having been at the pains of preparing an elaborate exposition of the railway views for the public in a condensed form, I propose to deal with the arguments expressed by that gentleman later on. For the present, I will confine myself to the evidence. The first witness was Mr. Grierson, general manager of the Great Western Railway Company.

MR. JAMES GRIERSON.

"Q. You are general manager of the Great Western Railway?

"A. I am.

"Q. What in your view would be the result of Mr. Hunter's opinion, that the rates should in all cases be equal, except by the express sanction of the Railway Commissioners?

"A. If his view were adopted, it would entirely annul the contract between Parliament and the Railway Companies, on the faith of which the latter have expended a large amount of capital. Further, the effect of such legislation would be either that practically there would be no differential rates made, or that Railway Companies would be carrying on their business at the greatest possible disadvantage, their time being occupied continuously before the Railway Commissioners.

MR. GRIERSON, GREAT WESTERN RAILWAY.

"Q. The very gist of the evidence before the committee was the differential rate?

"A. If that is the only charge against the Railway Companies, then I would venture to say we have acted upon the special authority, indeed instructions, of Parliament, and that we have not made these differential rates merely at the whim and fancy of the Railway Company, but that we have obeyed the desire of the public It is they who come and ask us to make a differential rate; the Railway Company does not go and propose it itself. A trader goes to the company and says, 'I can do a certain business, if you can make a certain rate; but I have competition to meet by water, or from a district elsewhere, which I cannot meet if you do not make me a special rate.'

"Q. Are you aware that there is a contract annually entered into between the traders in the Eastern States and the Railway Companies; for instance, between the Pittsburgh manufacturer and the Pennsylvania Railways?

MR. GRIERSON, GREAT WESTERN RAILWAY.

"A. I will take it from you that it is so.

"Q. Would you take it from me that these rates are fixed for a twelvemonth in advance, and that they are mileage rates?

"A. I will take it from you.

"Q. Will you also take it from me that that system is attended with every satisfaction to the traders and also to the Railway Companies?

"A. May I ask if it is a universal mileage rate?

"Q. It is a graduated mileage rate, diminishing as the distance increases.

"A. Such arrangements might suit a Continent like America, but it would create quite a revolution in this country.

"Q. At present there is no such mileage system in this country?

"A. No.

"Q. Therefore, I may take it that we should regard the Railway Companies as a sort of special providence to bring up the less favoured districts to the position of the more favoured ones?

"A. Special providence would be your term, and not mine; but I would say that we have met the requirements of the country, and have furthered the interests of trade by the way in which the rates have been framed. Still, I do not attribute that all to the Railway Companies; it is from information afforded to us by the traders that the rates have been framed.

Mr. Grierson, Great Western Railway.

"Q. You believe that the policy of the Railway Companies has been most advantageous to the trade of the country?

"A. Most clearly.

"Q. Do you think, for instance, that there is no ground of complaint on the part of the agriculturists that their produce should be carried between two termini at a very much higher rate than produce imported from abroad?

"A. If you refer to the question of meat, you may take that as a special case; and I may admit that I would not be prepared to defend every rate in force, even upon the Great Western Railway. There must be rates which it may appear ought to be revised, no matter how the scale is fixed.

"Q. Perhaps you will kindly turn to the first page and take the maximum rate for coal. From South Staffordshire to Banbury, the rate is 5s. 2d.; from South Staffordshire to Aynhoe, which is six miles more, the rate is one penny less?

"A. I am bound to say that I cannot understand it, if it is so. If it is so, I call that an error; but I will ascertain whether it is so or not.

"Q. Whether it be an error or not, it would operate prejudicially to the Banbury trader?

"A. You may take it that if this is accurate; it is a mistake in fixing the charge.

"Q. If it is an accurate statement, it shows that there are differential rates to one place against another?

"A. In the case of beer it is so. Every one knows of the Burton agreement between the London and North-Western Railway Company and the brewers, to give the Burton brewers very low rates.

"Q. In point of fact, a preference in favour of the brewers?

"A. It is so; but that is a very large trade.

"Q. Now, with reference to the rates for coal, Mr. Baxter stated that in July, 1871, the Great Northern Railway Company carried coal to London for 6s., and in 1873 the charge was 9s. 9d. I asked him why the difference was so large; and he stated that in 1871 there was what he called a duel between the Great Northern and the Midland Companies, and they fought it out in this way—

they took no reduction of rates. So you observe that in 1871, when there was competition between two large Railway Companies, the coal was carried at 6s. a ton; and in 1873, when the two companies were combined, the coal was carried at 9s. 9d. Which should you say was the most beneficial to the public, the combination or the competition?

MR. GRIERSON, GREAT WESTERN RAILWAY.

"A. The consumer gets the benefit of that competition, but it cannot be a benefit to the public that the Railway Company should carry goods at a dead loss.

"Q. What would it matter to the public whether the Railway Company carried at a dead loss or not?

"A. The public are very much interested in the Railway Companies being in such a financial condition that they can meet the requirements of trade in the way of making a reduction on that kind of trade which will not bear the full rate.

"Q. You think it of interest to the public that the Railway Companies should combine to arrange their charges rather than compete with each other?

"A. *I say competition, in a certain sense, is utterly impossible between two Railway Companies.* In the days of coaching proprietors, when one man

MR. GRIERSON, GREAT WESTERN RAILWAY.

started with £5000 and another with £3000, and they went on with competition, of course the man with £5000 had the benefit of having the whole trade to himself as soon as the other one was run off the road. That is impossible with Railway Companies. It is impossible to close a railway, and it is impossible to make them bankrupt, so that they must arrange the rates. It would be as unreasonable to expect that after a competition, such as existed between the Midland and the Great Northern Companies, they would not raise their rates to a reasonable sum, as to expect that the Great Northern and North-Western Companies, who formerly carried passengers from Manchester to London for five shillings, should not go back to their fair rate.

"Q. You admit that the Railway Companies do arrange their rates?

"A. Yes, clearly."

It is necessary here to compare this evidence with that of Mr. Baxter, the celebrated railway solicitor, late of the firm of Baxter, Rose, and Norton, who gave exhaustive evidence on behalf of the Railway Companies.

Select Committee—Railway Evidence. 137

Mr. Baxter is asked—

"Q. I suppose nobody has had greater experience than yourself in passing Bills through Parliament?

"A. I have had some experience.

"Q. And I suppose the rates in those Bills have been fixed by your advice?

"A. No. They have a very old method, and a very unhandy method of fixing the rates. The mode of fixing the rates in Parliament might be much better done, but they have continued in the old groove, and practically the rates are of very little consequence in the present state of the country. The competition between the railways and the pressure on the part of merchants and consumers command the rates and regulate them altogether, irrespective of statutory enactments.

"Q. Do you think, altogether, that with the present rates it would be safe for Parliament to cut out the maximum rates altogether, and let the Railway Companies charge what they like?

"A. I think it would be quite safe to abolish all statutory rates whatever on railways, and let them charge what they can. *The competition is so perfect throughout the country*, and the pressure on the part of traders is so great, and the system so mature, that I think you might safely supersede all rates in Acts of Parliament, and give to the Railway Companies an absolute power of charging."

MR. GRIERSON (*continued*).

"Q. What is the wording of the Act of Parliament of 1863?

"A. The wording of one of the clauses is, "The rates between competitive places, such as London and Birmingham," and so on, "shall be equal."

"Q. Supposing you find a Railway Company going between two places within a certain distance of each other, and another going between the same places a considerably longer distance, both carrying at the same rate, are you not landed in one of two alternatives—either that the one going the shorter distance is making very much larger profit than ought fairly to be taken, or that the railway going the longer distance makes an excessive loss?

"A. It does not follow either that the one would be making an excessive profit, or that the other would be making an excessive loss, but each must be taken upon its own merits. As between London and Swansea, the London and North-Western Company would not make so large a profit as the Great Western Railway Company.

<small>Mr. Grierson, Great Western Railway.</small>

"Q. Then it might even be that the profit which the Great Western Company was making might be too large?

"A. I have not found that to be the case.

"Q. If the London and North-Western Company were making a profit, it is quite clear that the Great Western Company were making too much profit?

"A. The London and North-Western Company might make ten or twenty per cent., and the Great Western Company might be making thirty or forty per cent.

"Q. Now, I wish to ask you about the carriage of tea, about which Mr. Taylor stated some curious facts. He said he paid a rate of 45$s.$ per ton from London to Swansea; and from London to Exeter, which is the same distance, the carriage was 33$s.$ 4$d.$; and from London to Plymouth, which is fifty miles further, the carriage was 24$s.$ 2$d.$ Can you explain that anomaly?

"A. There is no doubt an apparent anomaly in

Mr. Grierson, Great Western Railway.

the rates, *but that arises from competition by sea.* We must either charge a competitive rate with the sea traffic, or give up the traffic altogether.

"Q. Is the 24s. 2d. on tea to Plymouth a remunerative rate to you?

"A. It will leave a small profit, but only a very small one.

"Q. If it leaves a small profit, it is perfectly clear that the rate from London to Swansea must leave a very large profit?

"A. It leaves a much larger one, no doubt; but it is perfectly obvious that a Railway Company could not exist if the traffic only yielded such a profit as that obtained from the tea between London and Plymouth.

"*Then, again, the question is, is the Railway Company to compete with the sea or not?* That is the simple question.

"Q. Supposing the Plymouth rate was not remunerative, would you not have to charge a higher figure to other places to which there was not sea competition, in order to make a profit?

"A. No, not if the traffic paid its expenses; but if the company suffered a loss by reason of that traffic, that certainly might be the case.

"Q. Do you think the company always competes with the sea at a profit?

"A. As I said before, it is difficult to say, unless the case was put before me in all its aspects. I would not like to say there are not cases in which the rates are too low; indeed, I think the Railway Companies have, in some cases as against the sea, unnecessarily reduced the rates.

"Q. Can you tell me on what principle rates are fixed at all?

"A. They are fixed, of course, in the first place, having reference to the power of the company to charge, and, in the next, as to the nature of the article—whether it is bulky or fragile, whether it is valuable, and whether there is competition by sea or by inland navigation; and, in fact, generally by what, under the powers of the company, the traffic will bear.

"Q. How do you ascertain what the traffic will bear?

"A. The public take very good care to let us know that. The goods managers of railways are in constant and continual communication with the traders. Of course, it is to the interest of the companies, as it is the interest of the traders, that

MR. GRIERSON, GREAT WESTERN RAILWAY.

Mr. Grierson, Great Western Railway.

there should be frequent communication upon a matter of that kind; it is to their mutual interest. The officers of Railway Companies are to a large extent educated by the traders in their business by their telling them what the nature of the goods is, and what the value of them is; what their competition as traders is. That is what every trader does. The goods manager makes use of the information which is given to him by the traders, and brings his influence to bear either upon his superior officer, if he has not full powers, or upon another company, if necessary, with the view of pulling the rate down, if the trader can satisfy him it ought to be done.

"Q. Would the raising or the lowering of the rates depend upon the trader's faculty for making complaints?

"A. I would not have used that word, but I would say, a mutual consideration of their interests.

"Q. Has it ever been the case, either in your company or any other, that railway officials have been interested in coal, and so on?

"A. I have known in small lines instances of persons acting for the company being interested in trade, but there is no such thing upon the Great

Western, nor upon any large and well-regulated Railway.

"Q. Has there never been any case upon the Great Western Railway where the railway officials have been interested in the rates?

"A. Are you referring to the Ruabon Colliery case?

"Q. I am not referring to any case in particular.

"A. I know a case in which certain officials of the Great Western Company invested in a Colliery Company, but they had no interest whatever in fixing the rates. I may say that I myself had no interest in that concern. You may take it from me, that if you had known anything of the working of large and properly managed lines, you would never have asked such a question.

"Q. Were not the prices charged for the conveyance of minerals and goods materially enhanced in 1873?

"A. They were.

"Q. And have not been materially reduced since?

"A. There were certain advances in certain places, but it was not a universal advance over the system.

Mr. Grierson, Great Western Railway.

Mr. Grierson, Great Western Railway.

"Q. Was not the advance general?

"A. Wherever we thought the traffic would bear an increase it was put on.

"Q. There were advances made?

"A. There were.

"Q. And they were made wherever you thought the traffic would bear it?

"A. Yes.

"Q. That is, wherever you thought you could squeeze it out of the traders?

"A. The public must pay; it must be got out of the consumers in some way.

"Q. It is not necessary that the public should always pay, as in the case of collieries, for instance. You know, a colliery will go on working at a dead loss, even when the public are getting the coal cheaply?

"A. The loss upon coal, as far as I understand, does not arise in any way whatever from the rates charged by the Railway Companies. The high prices of coal in 1873 and 1874 induced people in London and Lancashire to put money into new collieries in South Wales, which, if they had all been completed, would have raised 5,000,000 tons more of coal per year than had been raised in 1872.

Many of those collieries have been completed; and it is the competition now between the collieries themselves which has brought the price so low. If we were to reduce the coal rates to-morrow, it would not benefit the collieries.

Mr. Grierson, Great Western Railway.

"Q. Do you really consider the interest of the colliery proprietors in not making a reduction of the rate?

"A. I am speaking of the present circumstances; the non-profitableness of the collieries at the present time, does not arise in any way from the railway rates.

"Q. I did not say that it did. I asked whether it would be to the advantage of the colliery owners to have the rates reduced?

"A. Then I say a reduction of sixpence a ton from South Wales to Birmingham would not benefit the colliery proprietors in the least.

"Q. Do you not think it was rather an extraordinary thing to charge Mr. Hickman 1s. 7d. a ton for a mile and a quarter? Do you not think it was a case for a special rate?

"A. It seems a high rate.

"Q. Can you be surprised that Mr. Hickman cannot compete with other manufacturers?

L

MR. GRIERSON, GREAT WESTERN RAILWAY.

"A. I do not think it is quite right to bring a case of this kind here, and say that neither of the companies would meet him in the matter. He may have sent a small quantity as a test, and not applied again. If Mr. Hickman really wished to enter into an arrangement, he should have applied to our goods manager, or to me; but he has not done so.

"Q. If you read the evidence he has given, you will see that this would appear to have been going on for some time.

"A. Let me read a letter of his with reference to an answer he gave at No. 4438, which is as follows:—'When a private individual goes to a great Railway Company for redress of any grievance, if he says, "You are charging me more than the maximum rate for this or that," the Railway Company simply laughs him to scorn, as they know they have the power of oppressing him in all sorts of ways.'

"Q. You say there is no competition on the part of Railway Companies?

"A. There is a competition of accommodation, but they do not undercut one another in the rates.

"Q. They form a 'ring'?

"A. They arrange the rates. You will readily

understand that that must be so; it could not be otherwise.

"Q. It is not to the interest of the public, certainly, is it?

"A. The public could not expect anything else. If you mean that the Railway Company should carry at a loss, that certainly would not be to the interest of the public.

"Q. I think you stated yesterday that the great evil that lay at the root of all the trade at present, the coal and iron trade especially, was the severe competition one with another, and that the reduction of the railway rates would not materially assist them?

"A. It is so with production.

"Q. *So that you have upon the one side a severe competition among the traders, but upon the part of the Railway Companies the traders have none whatever?*

"A. They have this competition. The Midland Railway will do all they can to bring in coals from their district, the Great Northern will do the same from theirs, the London and North-Western from theirs, and the Great Western from theirs.

"Q. I am quite aware of that; but they will not

Mr. Grierson, Great Western Railway.

MR. GRIERSON, GREAT WESTERN RAILWAY.

alter the rates. I believe they have an agent who goes to each colliery district, and they do all they can to get the trade on their line, but that agent dare not offer any reduction of rates to do that.

"A. The canvasser could not go to the colliery proprietor and say his company would reduce the rates; the rates had been arranged beforehand?

"Q. The Great Western Company has bought up the Gloucester and Hereford Canal, has it not?

"A. The canal was forced upon us, I can assure you. It was not bought up with any desire on our part to have it.

"Q. Has not the action of the Great Western Railway Company, whether forced upon them or not, taken away the independent competition which Hereford would have had?

"A. They have had it up to to-day, and they have not suffered by it; it is working still.

"Q. Was not the canal closed upon the 1st of July?

"A. Notice was given to close it upon the 1st of July, but it is not actually closed."

Mr. George Findlay.

"Q. You are general manager of the London and North-Western Railway Company?

"A. I am.

"Q. Do you give preferential rates to the brewers?

"A. I scarcely understand the word 'preferential' in the sense in which you use it; but we give lower rates to Burton, as being a large place for the consumption of malt and barley, than we do to other places where so much brewing is not carried on.

"Q. Do you give them carriage at the rate of six quarters to the ton, whereas you charge to other places at the rate of five quarters?

"A. We do charge them at the rate of six quarters to the ton.

"Q. Then you admit you do give a preference to the brewers at Burton over the brewers at other districts?

"A. We give lower rates, and to that extent a preference over the brewers in other districts."

[With reference to this evidence, on a subsequent day, the witness made the following statement:—

"Before the committee ask me any questions, there are one or two little points I should like to clear up. The honourable member for Gloucester,

Mr. Findlay, London and North Western Railway.

I think it was, asked me a question when I handed in the Burton agreement, with reference to whether there was not a preference to the Burton brewers carrying six quarters to the ton as compared with actual weight to other brewers. I think I said that to that extent it was a preference to the Burton brewers; but I did not in the least intend to imply that, having reference to our agreement with Messrs. Allsopp and the general terms under which the Burton traffic was carried, it was an *undue* preference within the meaning of the Act of 1854 or the Act of 1873."]

MR. FINDLAY (*continued*).

"Q. Would you turn to the table put in by the Board of Trade, as I wish to ask you one or two questions upon it? Looking at page 8, I see that the charge for dung of all sorts shows there is a difference varying from 1s. 8d. to 3s. 8d. over the maximum mileage station to station rates. Take the case of Runcorn, for instance. The maximum rate in the company's Act for "dung," all sorts of manures, lime, stone for building and paving, slates, bricks, sand, and iron ore, is 1s. 3½d., and the charge by the company's rate book is 5s., making an excess over the mileage rate of 3s. 8½d. for, I presume, what you call terminals?

"A. Yes; the case of Runcorn is rather peculiar, because, in the construction of the Frodsham curve, which connects Frodsham with Runcorn, it was made obligatory upon the London and North-Western Company, as joint-owners of the Birkenhead Railway, to contribute the toll to the joint line, not as between Chester and Frodsham, but as between Chester and Warrington; and the rate was originally made applicable from Chester by Walton Junction, and then from Walton Junction upon the St. Helen's line and back over the Runcorn Bridge to Runcorn; and the rate has remained at the figure charged by that route, because, as I have said, it was made obligatory upon us to contribute in proportion to the joint line, as though it had travelled by that route. But, as a matter of fact, no traffic whatever has been carried at the 5s. rate; the only traffic which has been sent at all was a traffic in the mineral class of 101 tons of stone, and that was charged 3s., but even since that traffic has been carried the charge was reduced some three months ago to 2s. 6d. a ton.

"Q. It appears that to the various stations

Mr. FINDLAY, LONDON AND NORTH WESTERN RAILWAY.

between Chester and Rugby, the company charge from 4s. 6d. to 6s. 9d. in excess of the maximum mileage rate. What explanation have the company to offer for this additional charge?

"A. Those charges are to cover the terminal services, and that difference may be explained, in some cases, in this way. Take the cases of Whitchurch and Stirchley, two towns in Shropshire. The distance to those towns has been shortened by the construction of what we call the Whitchurch and Tattenhall Railway, and I have no doubt the rates were made applicable, not by the short route, but as by the route by way of Crewe, and so to Whitchurch and Stirchley.

"Q. The excess over the maximum mileage rate varies from 4s. 6d. to 6s. 9d., being an average probably of 4s. Do you consider that a reasonable charge for terminals on station to station goods, those being packed manures?

"A. I dare say for terminals they are rather high. Take the case of Rugby, where the difference is 6s. 9d. As a matter of fact, the rate which appears in the book .which is taken as a special class rate does leave a margin of 6s. 9d.; but no traffic of that kind has ever passed between Chester and Rugby, or is ever likely to pass.

"Q. If you take the first column on page 9, you will find the differences between column 1 and column 3 vary from 3s. up to 8s. 1½d., making probably an excess of 6s. over the station to station mileage rates. Do you consider that a reasonable sum to charge for terminals?

Mr. Findlay, London and North Western Railway.

"A. There is that difference, and I think it is not an unreasonable difference.

"Q. You do not think that for station to station goods, such as undamageable iron, sums varying from 3s. to 8s. 1½d. are an unreasonable charge for terminals?

"A. I say that if there were any traffic in most of those cases, special rates would have been quoted, but in a great many instances no traffic exists whatever. And, then, you have assumed that the special class rate, which include a great many articles which are not specified in the lowest rate for dung and compost, applies to all articles in the class.

"Q. You say it is very likely; it seems to me very unlikely that your rate book would not show the distances upon your own line.

"A. It probably would do so; but as it all turns upon this question, I want to make myself perfectly

MR. FINDLAY, LONDON AND NORTH WESTERN RAILWAY.

understood upon it by the committee, that a company may have a line between two given towns as straight as the crow can fly, and as straight as a line can be drawn, and, according to the Act, they are entitled to charge between those towns a certain mileage toll, whatever that may be. They may also have another route, which is some distance round about; the one may be the arc and the other the chord, and there may be nothing whatever, so far as the powers of the company are concerned, to prevent them, if they carry by the longer route, from charging by the longer route. I desire to impress upon the committee that there is nothing to compel the company to charge the public by the shortest route, if the traffic is carried by the longest route. I cannot illustrate that better than by saying, take the distance from Stafford to Rugby, which is fifty miles. If the traffic were carried as a matter of convenience to ourselves, and not at the public option, round by way of Birmingham, being taken twelve miles round, I have never heard it contended that we are not entitled to the tolls that we possess round by way of Birmingham. Because we possess two lines, we are not bound to charge the lowest toll, as for the shortest route

"Q. Now, taking the first-class goods, the difference between column 1 and column 4 varies from 1s. 8d., under the maximum mileage rate, up to 10s. 4½d., a fair charge for collection, delivery, and terminals.

Mr. Findlay, London and North Western Railway.

"A. May I ask to what station does the 10s. 4½d. apply?

"Q. Can you tell the committee what you pay for the cartage at Rugby and Chester?

"A. I should say that it costs about 2s. 6d. a ton at each end.

"Q. And the balance remaining over would leave 5s. 4d. for terminals?

"A. Yes, in that case it would be so; no doubt, there would be charges for clerkage, for loading and unloading, and for all services which you have mentioned.

"Q. Those services would be included in the terminal charge?

"A. Yes.

"Q. Then I see upon second-class goods to Rugby, the margin is as high as 11s. 4d.; does not that seem to be a very high charge for terminals and for collection and delivery, even assuming that you are entitled to claim for terminals?

MR. FINDLAY, LONDON AND NORTH WESTERN RAILWAY.

"A. It looks rather a high charge,

"Q. Now, taking the third class, the difference there for collection, delivery, and the terminals, so far as they are beyond the maximum rates, varies from 6s. 10d. to as high as 16s. 4d., and that class includes hides, green or market, and dry and loose; do you consider that a reasonable charge for terminals on hides?

"A. I think in regard to hides, it would be a reasonable charge—there is no doubt about that; but in those cases you have mentioned, practically there is no traffic.

"Q. Can you explain on what grounds you put such excessive charges in your rate books, when there is no traffic?

"A. It may be, if I had to revise the rates to-day, that those rates would be made more to assimilate. I am free to admit that there are many rates which do want assimilating within the powers which we claim of toll and terminal.

"Q. Now, coming to the fourth class 'manufactured,' do you see that the difference put down between column 1 and 3 (column 1 being the maximum rate by the company's Act, and column 3 what is charged in the company's rate book) varies from 16s. 6d. a ton to 24s. 9d., in excess of the maximum mileage rate?

"A. Yes; in that case the traffic all comes in in lots of less than 500 lbs.

"Q. But let me point out that that is not an excuse for having in your rate book an excessive charge?

"A. It assumes that it is an excessive rate, having regard to the services which are performed with respect to the fourth-class traffic. I may say I believe that with regard to a large proportion of the traffic of the fourth and fifth classes, scarcely any terminal that you would consider would be a reasonable sum would pay for the services we have to perform for it. Mr. Grierson gave, as an illustration, chairs and tables, and other traffic of that kind, showing that scarcely any chargeable terminal for that traffic would pay.

"Q. Do you take up this position, that for goods in ton lots, which is the quantity we may infer they are carried in, those goods would be charged sums varying from 15s. 6d. to 24s., in addition to the mileage rates; and do you consider that this is a reasonable rate?

"A. Yes, I think so; because this traffic does

Mr. Findlay, London and North Western Railway.

Mr. Findlay, London and North Western Railway.

not go in ton lots, and that rate would apply to one ton, or to any weight above 500 lbs. It is a matter of fact that that traffic does not go in large quantities.

"Q. But as it appears from the rate book, your charge for collection and delivery of furniture and terminals is as much as from 32s. to 41s. in excess of the maximum mileage rate?

"A. Yes; and I think that a reasonable charge; that will be about 15s. at each end.

"Q. You consider those to be reasonable charges?

"A. Yes; for that class of traffic."

Mr. Henry Tennant.

"Q. You are the general manager of the North Eastern Railway Company?

"A. I am.

"Q. I think you admit that you give the public a large advantage in forwarding foreign cattle over home cattle?

"A. We give a differential rate.

"Q. Is the differential rate in favour of foreign cattle, or against the traffic in foreign cattle?

"A. It is in favour of foreign cattle in this sense, that it is lower than we charge from Newcastle for the home-fed stock.

"Q. Then do I understand that there are two distinct rates—an import and a local rate?

"A. There are two distinct rates—an import rate and a local rate.

"Q. Can you reconcile your action with the requirements of the second section of the Railway and Canal Traffic Act of 1854. Does that section require that 'No such company shall make or give any undue or unreasonable preference or advantage to or in favour of any particular person, or company, or any particular description of traffic in any respect whatsoever; nor shall any such company subject any particular person, or company, or any particular description of traffic to any undue or unreasonable prejudice or disadvantage in any respect whatsoever'?

"A. The governing words are 'undue or unreasonable.' You may read that section as indicating that a Railway Company may give a preference or an advantage, the only reservation is that *it shall not be undue or unreasonable.*

"Q. *Do you consider that it is not an undue*

MR. TENNANT, NORTH EASTERN RAILWAY.

advantage to convey foreign cattle at lower rates than the home cattle?

"A. I do not think it is either undue or unreasonable.

"Q. At all events, that is your interpretation?

"A. That is my view upon it.

"Q. Is it the case, that you have the highest rates in the kingdom for artificial manures?

"A. I should think very likely it is. I do not know what every other company's rate is; but I should think it is very likely as you say.

"Q. You do not know of any other company which is entitled to charge higher rates than you do?

"A. Not higher than we are entitled to do.

"Q. Do you not charge as high as you are entitled to do?

"A. I think not.

"Q. We have it in evidence that you are charging 3d. upon distances over fifty miles, and 3½d. for distances under fifty miles, on artificial manure?

"A. I think that is a mistake. I have not seen any evidence to that effect.

"Q. Do you deny this to be the fact?

"A. I think we do not charge our maximum rates above fifty miles.

"Q. Nor under fifty miles?

"A. I should say that in a considerable number of cases under fifty miles, we do not charge our maximum rates either.

"Q. Will you explain by what Act you got authority to charge these additional rates for manure?

"A. I think the Act authorizing the rate was passed in 1865.

"Q. That was subsequent to the amalgamation of the lines which you were telling us about some time ago.

"A. Yes, it was.

"Q. Then, I suppose, the committee of 1872, if the rate for manure is higher than before the amalgamation, were in error in respect to that particular article?

"A. I suppose they spoke of it generally, from the evidence which had been given.

"Q. What was that Act principally for to which you referred; had it anything to do with your main line, except in the matter of these rates?

"A. I think there were several things in it;

Mr. Tennant, North-Eastern Railway.

Mr. Tennant, North-Eastern Railway.

there was the construction of some short branches, for one thing. But I have not got the Act here.

"Q. What was the name of it?

"A. The Pelaw Branch Act, speaking generally.

"Q. The Act professes to be principally an Act for enabling you to construct about eight or nine small branches in connection with the North-Eastern Railway Company, does it not?

"A. It was a kind of omnibus Bill.

"Q. The notice of the Bill is headed, 'Powers to Construct Railways between Pelaw and Lyne Dock, and to extend the Lyne Valley Railway,' and so on; 'and for the amendment of Acts and other purposes.' I wish you to read to the committee the Parliamentary notice in respect to the alteration of the rates, so as to show the notice the public had of this intended increase of rates" (handing a volume to the witness)?

"A. The notice was in the usual form, I suppose. After referring to several other things, it says, 'And also power to levy tolls, rates, and duties, for and in respect of the proposed railways and works; and to alter existing tolls, rates, and duties; and to confer such exemption from the payment of such existing and proposed tolls, rates, and duties as may be thought expedient.' This appears to be taken from the *London Gazette* of the 22nd of November, 1864.

Mr. TENNANT, NORTH-EASTERN RAILWAY.

"Q. Now, will you be good enough to read the clause in the Act which gives you this authority; this power is dealt with in a proviso to a clause, and not in a separate clause?

"A. It is clause 20 in the North and East Riding Pelaw and other Branches Act (1865). The first part of the clause sets out the tolls that may be taken with the proviso, 'Provided that as regards coal or coke sent as samples, in boxes or sacks, or in any other manner than that in which coals and coke are ordinarily carried by the company, and also as regards guano and artificial manure, the company may, for the convenience thereof by them, or any of the railways, demand and take the same tolls as they are authorized by the North-Eastern Railways Act of 1854, to demand for the conveyance of merchandise, matters, or things not therein specially enumerated.'

"Q. The Bill passed through Parliament as an unopposed Bill, I think?

"A. Yes, it did.

"Q. Do you think the notice which you read

MR. TENNANT, NORTH-EASTERN RAILWAY.

was sufficient to inform the farmers of the north-eastern districts *that they were going to have their manure rates more than doubled?*

"A. That is in accordance with the notice prescribed by Parliament.

"Q. What appears to me to be remarkable about this clause is, first, that it is introduced as a proviso into a Bill which, upon the face of it, appears to be dealing with eight small branches of the North-Eastern Railway; and, second, can you offer any explanation as to why manure was not put into any nominal class, but put into the class of 'unenumerated articles'?

"A. I cannot give you any reason now for its being done in that way.

"Q. But, in point of fact, now you have power to charge for this guano and artificial manure at your highest rates?

"A. Yes; that is the effect of the clause.

"Q. We have heard a good deal about the trade being able to bear a charge; do you think the farmers can afford to bear such a charge as the highest rate for guano and artificial manure?

"A. I think they appear to bear the charges which the company make. It does not follow, because we have maximum rates, that in every case we impose them.

"Q. But I understand you were imposing the charge of 3½d. in most cases, for distances under fifty miles?

"A. I think that is a mistake."

MR. TENNANT, NORTH-EASTERN RAILWAY.

Mr. Charles Scotter.

"Q. You are the goods manager of the Manchester, Sheffield, and Lincolnshire Railway Company?

"A. I am.

"Q. Are you opposed to the principle of equal mileage rates?

"A. Yes.

"Q. Do you agree with Mr. Grierson, as to his view on the suggestion of charging equal profits per mile on the same class of goods?

"A. I entirely agree with Mr. Grierson.

"Q. And with regard to coal?

"A. I disagree entirely with the principle of charging equal rates upon any class of goods, whether merchandise or minerals. I agree with Mr. Grierson's views.

"Q. You hold that you would not be showing

MR. SCOTTER, MANCHESTER, SHEFFIELD, AND LINCOLNSHIRE RAILWAY.

an undue preference supposing there were two traders in Liverpool, one sending you a consignment of English and the other American cheese, both to be sent up to London, in charging a much higher rate in one case than in the other?

"A. Certainly not. I say there is nothing to prevent a Railway Company giving a preference. *That is a preference, but it is not an undue preference.*

"Q. What is the advantage gained by the short distance clause, put in at the instance of the Railway Companies?

"A. The advantage they gain is, that where you carry traffic over two or three miles, they have the power to charge a minimum of sixpence; but I say that minimum ought to be extended.

"Q. You do not vary your figures in winter, I believe?

"A. We do not advance our rates. For the last five years we have not advanced our rates at all; the whole of the rates of the country have been tending downwards. I think I am justified in saying *that the rates of the railways are lower now than they ever were.*

"Q. But what were you doing the five years before that?

"A. There were very few advances.

"Q. Everything has gone down in business, has it not?

"A. Yes.

"Q. And if business had gone up, you would have gone up too, would you not?

"A. We shall have to go up upon some traffic.

"Q. I suppose it is you who are responsible for fixing the rates on goods?

"A. I am.

. "Q. You say you take a great many things into consideration, among other things what the traffic will bear; how do you ascertain what the traffic will bear?

"A. The public interested in the traffic, merchants or manufacturers, come to my office and discuss the whole question; it is a matter of discussion and arrangement perhaps weeks before the rate is fixed.

"Q. And how do you ascertain what profit there is, or how do you find out whether the trade will bear it? Do you assess the freight?

"A. It is entirely a matter of conference

Mr. Scotter, Manchester, Sheffield, and Lincolnshire Railway.

between the Railway Companies and the public. If they make out a good case for reduction, and if the Railway Company see their way to make a reduction, we make it. In the large traffic we have to deal with iron, rails, ironstone, and all those sort of things. We know the price as well as the merchants themselves.

"Q. You assume to know what it costs the trader to produce the goods, and what profit he has; and you raise and lower your rates according as you think he can afford to pay?

"A. No; I say not according to the profit; that is only one small element.

"Q. Are you entitled to charges for shunting?

"A. Yes; certainly.

"Q. You say shunting is not incidental to conveyance?

"A. Certainly.

"Q. Can you convey the goods without shunting?

"A. Certainly.

"Q. Then, why do you do it?

"A. If a man brought us a load of goods properly formed and complete to be conveyed over the railway, then there is no shunting required.

"Q. I ask, can you convey goods without shunting?

"A. Some of them we can.

"Q. And some you cannot?

"A. And some we cannot.

"Q. And in that latter case, certain shunting would be incidental to the conveyance?

"A. Yes, it would."

Mr. Jabez Light.

"Q. I think you are the goods manager of the South-Eastern Railway Company? *South-Eastern Railway.*

"A. I am.

"Q. Do you admit that the rates are correctly compiled by Mr. Hunter?

"A. Some of them are. When I first saw them I thought it was not much use checking them, because I thought they were rather misleading than otherwise.

"Q. They cannot be misleading, when they are copied from your rate book?

"A. But, I say, the column of maximum charge, say from Folkestone to London, if so much, is misleading.

"Q. Do you say these statements from the rate book are not correct?

Mr.
Light,
South-
Eastern
Railway.

"A. I think they are not correct, because the figures themselves do not state whether they are station to station rates or collected and delivered rates.

"Q. Do you not quote the furniture rate as a collected and delivered rate?

"A. No.

"Q. Are you quite certain about that?

"A. I should not give such a positive reply unless I were. All the class goods, one, two, three, four, and five, are station to station, so far as our rate books are concerned. I only know that the public pay those rates as station rates, and if we do the collection and delivery, we make an extra charge, and they pay it.

"Q. If those are station to station rates, according to Mr. Hunter, your maximum rate for furniture, which you are entitled to charge from Dover to Folkestone, is 2s., and you are charging 19s. 2d.?

"A. Of course, Professor Hunter has used his own idea as to what our charges are, and he has made it 2s.; but I do not agree with him. But even supposing I did agree with him, I say there is no terminal charge which you can possibly make which will more than just cover your expenses and liability for the loading of furniture."

Mr. Archibald Scott.

"Q. You are general manager of the London and South-Western Railway?

"A. I am.

"Q. Do you not carry grain at 10s. 6d. to Nine Elms from Havre, and from Southampton at the same price, and therefore carry it virtually from Havre to Southampton for nothing?

"A. That is not so. The grain that we carry from France to London is barley; we carry nothing but barley, and of course there is so much competition by sea from France to London, that the rate is necessarily a low one.

"Now the rate from Havre to London for barley, in lots under ten tons, is 12s. per ton.

"Q. What is the charge for wine in casks from Havre to London? Is it 20s., including delivery?

"A. I should think it would be about that.

"Q. Could you tell me what the charge is for wine in casks from Southampton to London, exclusive of delivery?

Mr. Scott, South-Western Railway.

"A. I do not know that. We carry practically no wine from Southampton.

"Q. Will you take it from me that it is 20s. also?

"A. It is 20s. 3d. from Southampton to London, including delivery.

"Q. Upon what principle do you charge eggs 50s. from Cherbourg to Manchester, while you charge, from Southampton to Manchester, 68s. 4d.?

"A. I do not know that that is the rate from Southampton. There are no eggs sent from Southampton.

"Q. Is not that the charge in your rate books, 68s. 4d., for eggs from Southampton to Manchester?

"A. Possibly it may be.

"Q. You justify your system of charging lower rates on foreign produce than for home traffic, because it is to the advantage of Railway Companies to do so; is that the sole justification?

"A. No; *we put it upon the public ground as well.*

"Q. Is not that giving an undue preference to the foreign trader over the English trader?

"A. I think not.

"Q. Not by charging less for foreign traffic?

"A. No. I do not know what home traffic is

injured by so large a traffic being conveyed into England by the South-Western Company's steamers.

"Q. At a lower rate than for carrying home produce?

"A. There is no such home produce to convey, as far as we are concerned. I will just give you an illustration. The total traffic that we conveyed from France in the month of June last, that is, in one month, by our own steamers, was—fruit, 88,375 packages; sugar loaves, 13,500; 69,215 packages of butter; 10,045 packages of eggs (those were less than usual); and there were 52,700 packages of potatoes. Then, besides these, there are sardines, and different other things. Now, we have no such traffic to convey, we will say, from Southampton; this is traffic conveyed for the supply of England from France, and I do not see that it cuts out any traffic this country could supply.

"Q. Are you carrying that traffic at a profit?

"A. I am afraid we do not make much profit by our steamships.

"Q. If you are carrying that traffic at a profit, ought you not to reduce the charge for traffic from Southampton?

"A. If there were a similar traffic to go from

MR. SCOTT, SOUTH-WESTERN RAILWAY.

Mr. Scott, South-Western Railway.

Southampton, no doubt we would make rates to suit the traffic.

"Q. Then, it is in consequence of the quantity that you make rates at a lower figure?

"A. There is no traffic from Southampton of this nature at all.

"Q. Then why do you classify it?

"A. Because under the classification the rates must be universal. But there is no butter and no eggs from Southampton.

"Q. Does not that arise from the fact that you are charging so much more from Southampton than you do from Havre?

"A. No; there is no such trade."

Mr. James Staats Forbes.

"Q. I believe you are chairman of the London, Chatham, and Dover Railway Company?

"A. I am.

"Q. And also of the Metropolitan District Railway?

"A. I am.

"Q. Would you say that most of the complaints which have been given in evidence before this committee arise from a desire for an advantage, either individually or locally, against other individuals or localities?

"A. That seems to me to be so.

"Q. Or the retention of natural advantages?

"A. That is what it is. If you lay down the principle that foreign hops are not to come over the railway at a less price than home-grown hops, you at once interfere with the varying circumstances under which commerce has to be carried on, because if you refuse to take foreign hops, the steamer will take them to London, and, therefore, the position of the local man is not in the least improved—he has that competition to face; and you, or those who say that Railway Companies should not avail themselves of every source of profit, are throwing them in this position.

"Q. But you noticed that the tendency of the evidence showed that those gentlemen who complained rather pointed to your lowering their rates, and not to the raising of the foreign rates? What they would say would be, 'We do not want to deprive you of the power of carrying hops from Flushing, but we want you to lower our rates to the same level.'

"A. Of course, that is the philosophy of the

MR. FORBES, CHATHAM AND DOVER RAILWAY.

complaint. Because you do something for somebody else in a different position from me and upon different terms from me, why should you not do it for me? That is what they all wish for; but, in my opinion, it would be impossible for a Railway Company to conduct its business upon a uniform rate, and this is only a uniform rate under another guise. Anybody with any experience must see that the theory of uniform rates is immediately exploded in practice.

"Q. The evidence given by the Kentish farmers was that the London, Chatham, and Dover Railway was exceeding the rates authorized by Act of Parliament?

"A. The farmers do not complain about it; we heard no complaints at all until certain people taught the farmers upon unfounded statements to think so. It is just the same with Mr. Massey. He thought he knew what he was saying; but the British farmer is more dense, a good deal, than Mr. Massey, and more likely to be misinstructed. Mr. Massey, who is a very intelligent man, took a good deal for granted, and so do these gentlemen who have taught the Kentish farmer to believe that which was entirely unfounded.

"Q. Was not it the contention of the farmers that you were carrying foreign produce to their prejudice?

Mr. Forbes, Chatham and Dover Railway.

"A. I have never seen any farmer making a complaint. I have heard the evidence of Professor Hunter.

"Q. Mr. Samuel Skinner said he came from Maidstone, and was asked by the Farmers' Club to come; and then he is asked, 'Are you aware of the maximum rate upon the South-Eastern and London, Chatham, and Dover Railways?' to which he replied 'No.' 'Q. I think you may take it from me, as Professor Hunter has given it, that the maximum rate upon all classes of goods is 13s. 8d. from the Bricklayers' Arms Station to Maidstone, and I presume it would be the same from Maidstone to the Bricklayers' Arms, and yet you say that they charge you on fruit 20s. a ton? A. That is so. Q. And upon hops they charge you 32s. 6d.? A. Yes. Q. It would follow that both those charges are considerably over the maximum rates? A. Yes. Q. Those charges, as I understand, include delivery? A. Yes, they do.' That is the sort of evidence to which the honourable member is directing your attention.

N

MR. FORBES, CHATHAM AND DOVER RAILWAY.

"A. I should be very happy to go through the evidence, but you must take it from me that so and so is so and so.

"Q. The charge against you, and which you very much admit, is that you carry for the foreigner at 25s. for 155 miles, and that you carry for the home producer at 30s. for 44 miles?

"A. I protest against its being supposed that I admit that, because I say you must compare like with like. I pointed out that the hops, because they were hops, carried *via* Flushing were carried under totally different circumstances from the hops carried in Kent; and, therefore, I say again, that I do not admit that you are doing the hops grown in Kent any harm, if you are carrying foreign hops at 25s., but it must not be taken that I admit that.

"Q. That is the farmer's complaint, as I understand?

"A. No doubt he may make that complaint.

"Q. Can you tell me the precise words of the clause upon which you found your right to charge for terminals?

"A. That is the East Kent Railway Act of 1853.

"Q. I wish to have upon the notes the words

upon which you rely for your authority to charge terminals?

"A. It says, after reciting the ordinary toll clauses, 'That the maximum rate of charge to be made by the company, including the tolls for the use of the said railway and branches, and of carriages, and for locomotive power and every other expense incidental to such conveyance (except a reasonable charge for loading and unloading goods, where such service is performed by the company), shall not exceed the amount mentioned in the following table;' and then it gives the tolls.

"Q. What are the words which you rely upon for authorizing your terminal charge?

"A. The maximum rates of charge alluded to are to cover every charge incidental to such conveyance, except a reasonable charge for loading and unloading, where such service is performed by the company.

"Q. Then it would be under the phrase, 'except a reasonable charge for loading and unloading'?

"A. Yes, and provided the charges were incidental to conveyance.

Mr. Forbes, Chatham and Dover Railway.

"Q. Are those the only words you have got?

"A. Yes; they are the only words we have got in this particular Act.

"Q. I think you stated that you issued last year a circular to the hop growers, stating you would carry hops only on the conditions stated in that circular?

"A. Yes.

"Q. In your evidence on the last occasion, you told the committee that your notice was that you would not receive the hops at all upon the conditions suggested in the *Mark Lane Express*, but upon the conditions you yourself had laid down?

"A. We received them upon the conditions of that notice, therefore I was quite right in what I said.

"Q. Upon what conditions did you receive them?

"A. Upon the conditions of the notice that we gave, and that notice was handed to the growers.

"Q. If you only received them upon those conditions, I suppose you declined to receive them upon the conditions suggested in the *Mark Lane Express?*

"A. Of course, we did not receive them upon the conditions suggested by the *Mark Lane Express*, because we were at variance with the *Mark Lane Express* as to the inapplicability of the conditions.

Mr. Forbes, Chatham and Dover Railway.

"Q. What conditions specified in the notice of the *Mark Lane Express* are inapplicable or illegal?

"A. The notice is as follows:—'The consignor requires the undermentioned consignment of hops to be carried, according to actual weight, from —— station to —— station in London. He does not require the company to load or unload these hops, or to deliver them in London, but he will perform these services by himself or agents.'

"Q. What part of that arrangement was it illegal for the consignor to demand?

"A. There is no question of legality or illegality raised.

"Q. I would ask you this question. Was it quite lawful for a consignor to ask you to receive hops upon the conditions specified in this notice?

"A. I suppose it would have been.

"Q. Did you decline to receive them?

"A. No; we declined nothing. We accepted the hops, and carried them.

"Q. Did you take them from station to station, or did you deliver them?

"A. We delivered them.

"Q. Then you did not carry them upon the conditions specified by the circular?

"A. *We did not, because they were not the conditions applicable at the time to the transit of hops.*

"Q. Is it your opinion that the Railway Companies are entitled to lay down any condition they think proper for the conveyance of traffic upon the line?

"A. If they are reasonable, under the circumstances, I say, yes."

From this it may be gleaned that the Railway Companies contend that they have a right to charge the maximum rates allowed by law, however high and unreasonable they may be; but should it so happen that any of these rates have (in their opinion) been fixed by Parliament at too low a standard to be remunerative, they have a right to make them so. That is to say, that instead of adding a "reasonable terminal," they add a terminal which makes a "reasonable rate," or, in other words, they charge the traffic "what it can bear." Again, the fact that high and illegal charges appear on the rate books is hardly excused by the announcement that there is comparatively "no traffic;" the wonder is that there is any!

STATEMENT OF SIR THOMAS FARRER.

I NOW come to the preferential system, as explained in the manifesto of Sir Thomas Farrer, Bart., and which consists of an elaborate defence of that system on the following grounds, viz. :—

1st. That it is an excellent institution, not only in regard to the interests of railways, but in that of the public.

2nd. That it is competition in the truest sense.

3rd. That if it did not exist, many people, if not whole districts, would be deprived of the necessaries of life, or have to pay much higher for them.

The statement being extremely lengthy and rather disjointed, I propose to deal merely with certain paragraphs, sufficient to give, in my opinion, an accurate idea of the line of argument employed, and which, for the sake of convenience, I have numbered.

No. 1.

The question which we have to consider is, whether the reasons which do exist or may exist in all these cases, viz. the attraction of traffic which, but for the lower rate, either would not exist at all, or would go by a rival route, is a sufficient reason to justify a lower rate, without at the same time requiring the companies to lower all their other rates, in cases where no such reason exists, to the same level. Now, the first observation upon this question is that if the Railway Companies are not allowed to attract custom and make profit in this way, they will be treated differently from any other traders. No one complains of a merchant or manufacturer because he makes more profit out of one class of dealings than he does out of another. But, it is said, the Railway Companies have Parliamentary privileges, and are monopolists. Unfortunately for this argument, the fact in this particular case is that they are not monopolists. Competition of routes or of markets is, *ex hypothesi*, what causes them to make the lower charges. The complaint, it must be remembered, is not that the charges are absolutely too high, but that the charges made to some are higher than those made to others, and the fact is that the lower rates are caused not by monopoly, but by competition.

SIR THOMAS FARRER.

In reply, I must remark, in the first place, that there appears to be a little conflict of opinion between Sir Thomas and Mr. Grierson on the subject of railway competition. The latter gentleman distinctly states that competition between railways is impossible, and that it is in the interest of the public that Railway Companies should combine and arrange their rates instead of competing with each other. Secondly, I allow that the public do not complain that merchants and manufacturers make more profit out of one transaction than another, for the simple reason that if their aggregate profits merely amount to a livelihood (much less a fortune), there are any number of people ready to step in at a moment's notice and compete with them. In the case of the Railway Companies, however, similar competition is at present perfectly impossible.

No. 2.

Sir Thomas Farrer. But English Railway Companies are, in the matter of goods traffic at any rate, generally exposed to severe competition.

In the first place, there are, to most centres of production and consumption, competing railways. It is true that there is a combination amongst Railway Companies as amongst other traders, and that they agree upon their tariffs; but they compete in speed and in convenience, which are money, and no agreement for an extravagant tariff is likely to stand long.

In the second place, there is the potential competition of new railways, which, as the Hull and Barnsley case shows, is not even now a *brutum fulmen*.

If Sir Thomas had been as discursive on the subject of new railways as on other points, he might have informed his readers that the Hull and

Barnsley is the only independent competitive line which has been commenced in England for more than twenty years; that Hull has been struggling in vain for a quarter of a century without success to obtain a competing line with the North-Eastern; that the whole of West and South Yorkshire has been injured during that period to an incalculable extent; and that in consequence of the Hull and Barnsley not being yet finished, the Sheffield steel trade is threatened with extinction. That the once flourishing town of Dronfield has been almost depopulated by the removal of extensive iron works to the sea coast, driven there by excessive railway rates; also, that the Hull and Barnsley Act was only obtained after public attention had been directed to the question in a more than ordinarily forcible manner, viz. by the subject being made *the question* at the last general election in Hull.

No. 3.

But there is in this country one form of competition for goods far more important, more far-reaching, and more unassailable than any of these—I mean competition by sea. There is direct sea competition between all the places situate on or near the sea coast of the United Kingdom. But this, extensive as it is, is only a part of the competition of which that great freetrader, the sea, gives us the benefit. There is competition for all imported or exported goods from any

SIR THOMAS FARRER.

seaport within reasonable distance to and from every inland place of importance, sometimes even across the inland to places on the opposite coasts; and this competition turns all railways which converge on a given point from opposite directions in competing routes. The Tyne, the Humber, the Thames, the Severn, the Mersey, and many other ports and estuaries, are places of export and import for all the internal traffic of the country; and the railways which lead to and from these ports join with the shipowners in keen competition for that traffic. There are few places in the country where such competion does not exist, and wherever it does exist, Railway Companies in fixing their rates are not their own masters, but are as strictly limited in their price as any trader is in selling cloth or sugar. If they charged more, they would lose the traffic. Competition may, then, be said to be the rule and not the exception, and it is the lowering of the rates caused by competition of which complaint is made. If this is so, it is certain that to prevent companies from thus lowering their rates would be to do what is not found expedient in the case of any other traders.

And, according to Sir Thomas, " the great free-trader, the sea," should be crushed as far as possible by the Railway Companies being allowed to perform the operation, not at their own expense, but at the cost of any traders who happen to be at their mercy. For instance, the money derived during the process of destroying the Staffordshire iron trade by the exaction of killing rates, should be devoted to the purpose of ruining the free-trade shipowners!

No. 4.

If we consider carefully what the position of these parties is, not absolutely, but relatively, to the rivals of whose preferential treatment they complain, we shall see that the introduction of railways has not made their position worse than it was without the railways, or that it would be now without them. On the contrary, railways have actually improved their relative position. So long as heavy goods had to be carried by road, places which had the advantage of sea traffic command the market; and so they would do again if railways were abolished. If neither corn nor cattle could be carried from different parts of England to London by rail, the wheat and cattle sent by sea to London would compete with corn and cattle from the interior of Great Britian more successfully than they do now. American corn and meat, Russian wheat and Danish cattle, would be better able to undersell the produce of English farms than they now are, if the latter had to be sent to the great centres of consumption by road.

This means, that if all other countries were provided with railways, and there were none in England, that traders in the latter country would be at a disadvantage in trade. We are, however, fully alive to this, and also to the further fact that if other countries were provided with heavy guns and ironclads, and England only possessed the bows and arrows and boats of bark of the ancient Britons, she would be at a disadvantage in war. Truisms of this sort, although interesting and instructive at a certain period of life, are more adapted to an elementary history of England or children's primer than to a discussion of this kind.

No. 5.

SIR THOMAS FARRER. In giving places which have the advantage of sea communication lower rates than they give where there is no sea competition, Railway Companies are therefore not creating an artificial preference, but only preserving to the former some part of the so-called natural advantages which they formerly enjoyed, and of which railways have partially deprived them.

This would seem as if, previous to the advent of railways, the population of these islands must have clustered round the sea-coast; but, as a matter of fact, we find that nearly all the great centres of industry were scattered all over the country, and that traders were apparently quite able to protect themselves against the natural advantages possessed by their competitors near the sea. This seems to show that if the trader is left to his own resources, he will probably discover the particular locality in England best suited to his own requirements. On the other hand, the system advocated by Sir Thomas simply puts the extinguisher on his judgment; for the most exhaustive calculations may be upset in a moment by a stroke of the directorial pen.

No. 6.

Nor, again, if the companies were to be compelled to give equal rates to all, would the advocates of the change derive from it the advantages they suppose. It must be remembered that all it claimed, and all that can now be claimed, under the law of "undue preference," is equality. The companies cannot, without the grossest injustice, be forced to level down. There is no absolute legal limit to their charges, except the statutory tariff. In most cases where competition now leads them to give a very low rate, it would be to their interest, if equality were forced upon them, to level up, and the effect would be injurious all round, except to the competing route.

The traffic which is now carried at a low rate in competition with a sea route would be driven from the railway to the competing route, whilst the railway, if it is to make as much aggregate profit as before, must charge a higher rate than it now charges, on the traffic which remains to it. If, for instance, Parliament were to take from the South-Eastern Railway Company the power of charging on fruit and hops from Boulogne the lower rates they now charge, or are alleged to charge, the result would be that the French fruit and hops would reach London by water, and that the Railway Company, in order to recoup themselves for the loss of the French traffic, would probably charge more on Kentish fruit and hops. This charge the Kentish fruit and hops would be able to bear, because the price would be raised in the London market. The consumer would suffer, and no one would gain except the competing shipowner.

In reply, I would suggest that if the companies were to "level up" they would have to close their railways. Sir Thomas's "great freetrader, the sea," would deprive them of the larger portion of their traffic at once, and it can hardly be imagined that they could live on the remaining portion even during the brief period in which that portion could exist. By their own confession they now charge "what the trade will bear." How, therefore, could they raise the rates without destroying it?

No. 7.

SIR THOMAS FARRER. If Parliament were to say that the companies shall charge no higher mileage rates on fish brought from Ramsgate, or from Hull, or from Grimsby to London, than they do on fish brought from Scotland or Ireland, the effect would be either to send the Scotch and Irish fish by sea to London, or to prevent it going to London at all. In either case the supply of fish to the markets would be restricted, the price would be raised, and though the price would be raised, the English producer would not get the benefit of it; for the Railway Companies would be able to raise their rates on English fish, and would do so in order to recoup themselves for the loss of their Scotch and Irish traffic.

I cannot quite see what justification there is for the statement that the supply of fish in London would be restricted and the price raised. Does Sir Thomas mean to say that there is not enough fishable space between Hull and Grimsby and all other southern coasts to supply London with fish? or does he mean to say that there is not sufficient capital or enterprise amongst our shipowners to enable them to supply sufficient boats for the purpose?

We may take it for granted that a Londoner will derive the same amount of nourishment from a fish caught off Hull or Ramsgate as from a similar fish caught off Scotland, and that there are enough fish within fishable distance of the former places to supply him with a great deal more than he wants. It may be taken for granted that the cost of bringing fish from Hull or Ramsgate, either by rail or water, is less than the cost of bringing it from Scotland. In what way, therefore, can society gain by the fact that the Londoner is consuming fish upon which a totally unnecessary cost has been incurred, that cost consisting of the amount of the difference in expense between bringing fish from Hull and Ramsgate and bringing it from Scotland? No sophistry can explain away the fact that there is a loss somewhere, which falls either upon the Railway Company, the trader, or the public, and most probably upon all three.

o

No. 8.

SIR THOMAS FARRER.

I think we may conclude that the parties who complain of preferential rates have not been injured by the railway system; that they suffer no injury which does not arise in the ordinary course of trade; and that, so far as they are concerned, there is no case for such a revolution in railway practice as the compulsory imposition of equal rates. It is a much simpler task to show that the public benefit by the lower rates. It is the very A, B, C of economy, that competition is the surest means of reducing price. Where competition exists, legislation is superfluous. The laws of supply and demand do the business far more effectually.

It is certainly a simple task to prove that the public must gain by lower rates, and this fact, I believe, is not disputed by the "parties who complain of preferential rates." If I understand them, they complain not that certain rates are low, but that the cost of making them so is taken out of their pockets.

No. 9.

SIR THOMAS FARRER.

Let us take a simple case in illustration of these arguments. The railways bring coal from Durham to London, 260 miles, for 8s. 7d. a ton, or 0·39 of a penny per mile. They bring a much larger quantity from Nottinghamshire, 140 miles, for 5s. 9d. a ton, or 0·48 of a penny per mile. They make some profit by the Durham traffic, or they would not carry it. They obviously make much more by the Nottingham traffic. The Nottingham coalowner is far better off than he was before railways were established or than he would be without railways. The London consumer benefits by the competition of the two coalfields and of the sea and railway routes. What, then, would be the effect of equalizing the rates? If, indeed, we could compel the railways to carry from Nottinghamshire at the Durham rate, we should, no doubt, get more out of them for less money. But this cannot be done under the doctrine of undue preference. All that doctrine can possibly justify is to compel equal charges. What would be the effect of equal charges in this case? It is obvious that the companies would level up. The result would be that no Durham coal would come to London by rail. The freight by sea from Durham might be raised, or it might not. If it were not raised, and if the coal now sent by rail went to London by sea, the only effect would be to transfer a certain profit from the Railway Company to the shipowner. If it were raised, the price of coal in London would rise; and the Railway Company, to recoup themselves for the loss of the Durham traffic, would probably raise their rate to the Nottingham coalowner.

My readers will recognize in this paragraph that our old friend Mr. Pease's district is referred to, and as they are already in possession of the facts and certain incidents relating to them, I need only say that my remarks relative to the fish traffic apply with equal force to the coal traffic. There exist in Nottinghamshire, Derbyshire, and Yorkshire enough collieries to block up London with coal if it were twice its present size, not to mention the seaborne coal from the North of

England. Now if, owing to equality in rates, the Railway Companies were to lose the carriage of coal from Durham to London, it follows that they would have to confine their attention to the carriage of the Yorkshire, Derbyshire, and Nottinghamshire coal to London, and, according to Sir Thomas, they would raise the rates in order to recoup themselves for the loss of the Durham traffic. But if they were to adopt this policy, it would simply be rendering it impossible that their own coal districts could compete against the seaborne coals. These districts can only just do so at the present rates, so that to raise them would simply amount to the Railway Companies playing entirely into the hands of the competing shipowners. Now, as a matter of fact (and very obviously so), the Railway Companies would adopt an exactly opposite course to that indicated by Sir Thomas. They would oppose the seaborne coal to the utmost extent of their power, by carrying from the Midland coalfields at the lowest possible rate consistent with profit; and the price of coal in London, instead of being raised, would be very materially lowered, to the advantage of all parties concerned. It is curious that Sir Thomas does not comment on the

Statement of Sir Thomas Farrer. 197

fact that a system which is, in his opinion, attended with such happy results to the public in its application from Mr. Pease's district to London, has never been adopted from London to Mr. Pease's district. What have the public in the north of England done that they should be debarred from the blessings of artificial competition which Londoners enjoy?

No. 10.

Sir Thomas Farrer.

Under these circumstances, if there is to be legislation on this subject at all, the justice and expediency of the case would probably be met by a provision requiring the companies, wherever a case of differential charge was proved, to give their reason for it. If the company could show that in the particular case the lower rate complained of was founded either on difference of cost or convenience to the companies, or on competition actual or probable, or on reasonable prospect of profit to the companies, these circumstances should be held to justify the lower rate. If they could not show any of these justifications, the Railway Commissioners should have power to put an end to the differential rate.

This means that the Permanent Secretary of the Board of Trade, a paid servant of the nation, with full knowledge of the evidence given by the public before the committee, has the effrontery to propose that Parliament should reply to that evidence by handing over the entire trade and agriculture of this country to the Railway Companies, to be dealt with as they may think fit.

This is the only logical inference which it is possible to draw from his suggestions; for were they adopted, no person in his senses could take action before the Railway Commissioners, neither could there be the slightest use in the continuance of their court.

I do not consider it necessary to give any more of Sir Thomas's arguments or recommendations; but in case I should have unwittingly omitted anything which might give a different complexion to his views, I beg to inform my readers that his statement *in extenso* appeared in the *Fortnightly Review* of August, 1882, which, curiously enough, is the organ usually adopted by his chief, Mr. Chamberlain, when publicly enunciating the discovery of new principles. The whole statement is simply a laboured attempt to prove that a most important item in the cost of production (viz. the rate of carriage) should be exempted from that competition which governs the cost of all the other items, and that, in lieu of that, the cost should be arbitrarily fixed by an irresponsible body of men. In dismissing this portion of my subject, I must remark that it would be interesting to ascertain if any Permanent Secretary or other person previous to the advent of railways (an institution, comparatively, of only the day before yesterday) ever pointed out that London was suffering from want of artificial competition; or that large districts in that city suffered from restricted food or other supplies, because the near markets were exhausted and the further ones incapacitated by the cost of carriage.

Now, if there is one characteristic more strongly marked than another in the railway evidence, Sir Thomas Farrer's statement, or the Select Committee's Report, it is the universal horror expressed at anything approaching an equal mileage system. The public would be injured, the railways would be injured, and no one would be benefited! The mere anxiety shown to impress this point upon the public mind indicates that the Railway Companies are fully aware that if equal mileage is adopted, their whole artificial structure will fall to pieces like a house of cards.

Taking the mileage system as proposed in the chapter on "Undue Preference" under the heading of "Suggested Remedies," let us see what kind of competition would result and the effects of it. Let us suppose the companies fix their rates too high, the great "freetrader, the sea," will very soon prove to them their mistake, by depriving them of a large portion of their traffic. It will then be a matter for them to decide what reduction to make, because on the amount of that reduction will depend the quantity of traffic they will get back from the sea carriers. Now, if they make their calculations correctly, they will be benefited by the lower rates and increased trade; and it also follows that every trader on their line (in the particular material) will also be benefited, because the reduction must apply to all equally.

Exactly the same advantage will occur to all parties concerned as happens when any ordinary trader decides upon extending his business. Say a linen manufacturer finds he can lessen the cost of production by increasing the quantity of it, he is naturally compelled to sell at a less price, in order to induce the public to purchase the increased quantity. He thus obtains an advantage by lessened cost and a larger business, and the purchasers of linen obtain another advantage, viz. the lower price they pay for it.

If ever England is to become prosperous again, she must enjoy the advantages of the kind of competition I have alluded to, and not to the so-called competition spoken of by the railway authorities and Select Committee, which is not only a palpable delusion and sham, but a system which in process of time would ruin any country in the world.

I have already mentioned some of the Acts of Parliament which refer to undue preference. I will now cite the judgment of Lord Chief Justice Cockburn in the case of Baxendale *v.* The Great Western Railway Company (5 Common Bench Reports, New Series, p. 336; and 28 Law Journal Common Pleas, p. 81) which is as follows :—

<small>JUDGMENT OF LORD CHIEF JUSTICE COCKBURN.</small>

It is abundantly clear from the statutory enactments which enjoin on Railway Companies obligation to afford accommodation on equal and reasonable terms, and from the provision of the statute by which jurisdiction is given to this court, against the affording of undue preference or the imposing of undue prejudice or disadvantage, that it was not the intention of the Legislature to leave to Railway Companies the unfettered exercise of their rights as proprietors of their respective lines, but, in return for the great powers which it has conceded to them, and for the monopoly of carrying on the business of the country, which in a great degree they have been enabled to acquire, has imposed upon them the obligation of affording accommodation on equal terms to the whole of the public. The policy and justice of such requirements are manifest, it being obvious that the

JUDGMENT OF LORD CHIEF JUSTICE COCKBURN.

powers of the Railway Company and its monopoly, under the impossibility of all competition, might afterwards be converted into a means of very great oppression by the company in point of charge, or in point of accommodation made in favour of one man at the expense of another, or by disadvantages in respect either of charges or accommodation imposed on one as compared with another; and it is plain that the oppressive effects of such inequality will be equally great, whether the motive be to benefit third parties or the Railway Company itself.

I would suggest that my readers should compare this judgment with paragraph No. 10 in Sir Thomas Farrer's statement.

There is also the case of Evershead v. the London and North-Western Railway Company (App. Cas., 2 Q.B.D., 254; 3 App. Cas., 1029), in which Earl Cairns, in giving judgment in the House of Lords, makes use of the following words:—

JUDGMENT OF EARL CAIRNS.

It appears to me that the question in cases like the present must always be simply this: Is the plaintiff in the action obliged to pay one sort of remuneration for services which the Railway Company performs for him, while the company performs the same services for other traders for either less remuneration or for no remuneration at all? My lords, in my opinion undoubtedly the Railway Company is—and that, indeed, is not disputed—in the collecting, loading, and delivering of goods, performing identically the same services for the plaintiff in this action as for the two other firms of brewers whose names have been referred to. Now, as a matter of policy and expediency, it may well be that the appellants have good reason for treating those other firms in the way they do; it may be that if they do not do that, these other firms, from the natural advantages of the situation which they have been able to occupy, will send their goods by another railway, and not by the railway of the appellants; but with those considerations the plaintiff in the action has nothing whatever to do. That is exactly one of those things which Parliament has *not* left open to the Railway Companies to judge of—whether in that way they will equalize in their capacity for competing with other lines or not. The one right—to my mind the clear and undoubted right—of a public trader is, to see that he is receiving from a Railway Company equal treatment with other traders of the same kind, doing the same business and supplying the same traffic. In my opinion, that is not the case with regard to this plaintiff, and therefore I think he is entitled to recover the monies he has paid under protest.

JUDGMENT OF EARL CAIRNS.

Lord Hatherley, following, says,—

According to the strict meaning of the Acts of Parliament as interpreted by the decisions, from the very moment that the company charges A a given sum when B, another person (a mere stranger up to that time, if you will), comes to the company to have the same services rendered under the same circumstances, he cannot be charged one farthing more than has been charged to A. He can only be charged precisely what the Act authorizes the company to charge, viz. that which has been charged to others; and the moment the directors take on themselves to charge less to another person, they must charge less to him, too. The charge must be the same to all for the same services performed in the same manner, for carrying the goods for the same distance, and for similar services rendered in every other way.

JUDGMENT OF LORD HATHERLEY.

Lord Blackburn, following, says,—

Judgment of Lord Blackburn.

The 90th section of the Railway Clauses Consolidation Act says, in what seems to me very clear terms, that 'All such tolls should be at all times charged equally to all persons and after the same rate, whether per ton, per mile, or otherwise, in respect of all passengers and of all goods or carriages of the same description, and conveyed or propelled by a like carriage or engine passing only over the same portion of the line of railway under the same circumstances.' I can hardly conceive clearer words than those to express the intention of the Legislature that there should be equality of charge in respect of all goods carried upon the same railway under the same circumstances.

These judgments clearly and definitely state what is the law with respect to undue preference. The railway authorities as clearly and definitely state that the law is *openly and deliberately set at defiance*. The Select Committee and the Permanent Secretary of the Board of Trade have joined with them in an organized attempt to talk down the law of the land in the supposed interest of Railway Companies. This procedure is a fitting example of the kind of treatment the public invariably receive when questions of this sort arise, and clearly shows that neither Parliamentary committees nor a Government which can allow the country to be mystified by the one-sided reproduction of the railway arguments *by one of its own officials*, can be trusted on this vital question.

THE THOUGHTFUL LIBERAL.

WHEN Lord Palmerston presided over the destinies of this country, his followers were contented to be called Liberals; but the supporters of Mr. Gladstone, or rather that portion of them whose highest political creed seems to be confined to a kind of fetish-like worship of that gentleman, are termed (or prefer to be termed) "thoughtful" Liberals. There is no denying that these individuals are endowed with a more than average amount of thought, but it is unfortunately unaccompanied by a corresponding amount of reflective power. Nature, however, seems to have partly atoned for this deficiency by endowing them with an overwhelming belief in themselves and their own intellectual capacities, to such an extent that they do not hesitate to set up and implicitly believe in theories formed on the experience of their few short years, when those theories are directly opposed to the principles by which mankind has hitherto been governed. Their individual views on nearly all subjects are diversified to the last degree, the only point in common being that they are invariably antagonistic to the decisions man has arrived at from an experience dating over ages of his existence. One advanced section will expatiate on the absurdity of monarchical government, whereas the smallest amount of reflection would show them that this form of government having been adopted almost invariably by the nations of the earth from the earliest ages, it is probable that mankind has seen some sufficient reason for its continuance, and that their tolerably patent objections may possibly have been observed even before the world had the advantage of the mature "thought" of the Radical of to-day.

Another section declaims against war in the abstract, and, with an amount of originality truly startling, will propose to do away with it by the substitution of arbitration. If the "thought" requisite for the evolution of this idea had been tempered with reflection, it would have been observed that there exists in the human breast such a thing as passion, which, although playing an important part in human affairs, is not always guided by true philosophical principles. It would have been seen that man is a combative animal, and that combativeness develops itself at a very early period in his career, so much so that children at school are at times in the habit of fighting, and that if they individually refuse when their turn arrives—preferring rather to offer a piece of cake as a conciliatory measure—the result is they lose their cake and eventually are probably kicked by every boy in the school, from the biggest to the smallest, and that a similar operation usually awaits the country which adopts like tactics. Also, it might have been observed that Nature, having implanted this quality in man, possibly foresaw the results which would follow, and took them into calculation, so far as they tended (together with the adjuncts of plague, pestilence, and famine) to keep the human race within certain proportions. But to do our modern Radical justice, although convinced that Nature's plan is barbarous, and of the necessity of altering it by the application of "thoughtful" minds to the subject, he is still fully alive to the evils of over-population, and to obviate them he has certain ideas on the advisability of limiting marriages, etc., etc., and is usually a devout believer in the doctrines of Malthus.

Reflection, however, would have shown him that population cannot be kept down by philosophical ideas, or the attempted inculcation of Malthusian doctrines, and that these arguments might with equal use be addressed to the conies on the rocks (or any animal blessed with the gift of fecundity), as that they will exercise the slightest effect on the curtailment of the production of the human species.

But it is to questions which relate to the possession of property that our "thoughtful" Liberal has chiefly directed his unreflective attention, and his views on this subject are so numerous, diversified, and subtle, that it· is impossible to describe them all. Suffice it to say that they include every possible dogma consistent with the confiscation of property, varying from the kind of limited ownership hinted at by Cabinet ministers (that is, ownership until deprived of it by Government) down to the boldly expressed opinions of the Democratic Federation, which denounce all capital as theft. Now, a moment's reflection must have shown our friends that property in some shape or form, from the earliest times, has been the reward derived by individuals in return for work performed by them in the interests of the community, from fighting its battles to cleaning its boots and shoes. To take away the reward, or even to destroy the advantages gained from the possession of it, would result in the destruction of the only incentive by which the individual is induced to minister to the welfare of the community at large, or, to use a common simile, it would remove the "bunch of carrots from the donkey's nose." A little more reflection would show them that for one country to put these confiscating notions in force whilst other countries did not, would result in the former becoming a wilderness, whilst the mere discussion of such ideas in authoritative quarters would greatly militate against its welfare.

Now the Radical is convinced that these ideas of his are new, whereas they are not only stale, but are as old as the hills. These people by some name or other have existed at all periods, and have usually been regarded as harmless, except upon the occasions in which they have attempted to reduce their principles to practice, when society has put them down in a more or less sharp and decisive manner. But our modern Radical's lines have been cast in pleasanter places, and although his ideas are not new, yet the mode in which they have been received, and more or less adopted by the responsible Government of a practical common-sense country like England, is very new indeed. What is newer still, is the fact that members of the Government often give the keynote to these views. A glance at the Parliamentary debates of 1883 will show how the time of the country was devoted to the discussion of these thoughtful fads.

As an instance, I may mention the lengthy debates which arose respecting the relative amount of pain endured by a pigeon shot at Hurlingham and a grouse shot in Scotland, the question being extended to a comparison of the amount of physical suffering endured by a fox when followed by hounds. One gentleman of the truly "thoughtful" type arrested the business of the country by narrating to the House how he once went out hunting, and told a falsehood to the master of the hounds out of sheer sympathy with the fox. The fact that tens of thousands of his fellow-countrymen obtain health and recreation from hunting, and that thousands more directly or indirectly derive their daily bread from it, was as nothing in the estimation of this gentleman compared with the comfort of a fox. He and his friends would put down hunting and shooting out of professed sympathy with the fox or the farmer, but really because they are the amusements of the comparative rich, forgetting that every act of this kind tends to drive those persons to foreign countries for their amusements, and that their money goes with them.

The incident I have referred to merely illustrates the kind of sympathy possessed by the modern Radical for everything and everybody in preference to his fellow-countrymen. Should a question arise between England on the one hand, and either Autocratic Russia or Republican France on the other, how invariably it happens that the expressed sympathies of the Radical are with those countries and against his own! We have lately seen India thrown into a state of ferment from one end to the other by a Radical governor-general (following the instincts of his kind) gratuitously placing the liberties of British subjects at the mercy of Hindoos and professional perjurers.

But, as I have before stated, the keynote to these ideas is often struck by members of the Cabinet. Thus, we have Mr. Chamberlain, who, whilst enjoying the dignity and emoluments appertaining to a seat in the Cabinet, is constantly posing before that portion of society called (by Mr. Bright) "the residuum" as the man who at a moment's notice is prepared to lead them. He boldly announces himself as an advocate of manhood suffrage, and the payment of members of Parliament; that is, he proposes that the taxpayer of this country should be called upon to pay the stump orator to legislate for him. Then, in audible "asides," he points to property in general, and land in particular. He speaks of the way in which the rich spend their money, of people who neither toil nor spin, of "unearned increment;" and as fast as he delivers himself of this pernicious twaddle, it is re-echoed by Mr. Michael Davitt and the members of the Democratic Federation. He is, in other words, trying to give us American institutions, minus the security to property which those institutions afford; for in the land of the almighty dollar, if a statesman of the Birmingham type were to go about the country directing the attention of the mob to the fortunes of the Astors, Vanderbilts, etc., etc., it is within the bounds of possibility that he would find himself in the nearest horsepond. For it must be remembered that Mr. Chamberlain has done more than generalize, in that he has absolutely singled out the leader of the Conservative party in the House of Lords, and directed public attention to him as an instance of a man who neither toils nor spins, at the same time omitting to state that Mr. Gladstone is another instance of exactly the same thing. Now, this either means that Lord Salisbury is wrong in living on the proceeds of his property, and that Mr. Chamberlain is the man to set the matter right, or it simply means a miserable attempt to set class against class, by appealing to the worst prejudices of the most ignorant portion of the community.

Now, who is Mr. Chamberlain that he should say these things? It appears that he is a gentleman of large fortune, and how he became possessed of it I will relate. My readers have doubtless heard of American "corners." They are formed by speculators taking advantage of certain states of the market, and acting in concert for the purpose of buying up large quantities of any material which is essential to the public use, and by creating an artificial scarcity they are enabled to obtain the absolute control of the market. Having secured it, their object is to sell the material to the public at any price they may choose to fix,—an object in itself perfectly legal, but in practice probably the most unlovely way of making money which can be conceived. Now, Mr. Chamberlain, or his father, or both, were engaged in the screw trade, and the idea seems to have occurred to either one or the other that by going round to all the people who had patents for the manufacture of screws, and by quietly buying them up, they could corner all the traders who were dependent on these articles, and could compel them to purchase their supply from Messrs. Chamberlain at exorbitant prices, far in excess of their intrinsic value. In the manipulation of this manœuvre they appear to have been eminently successful, and the fortune of Mr. Chamberlain is the result. Upon the "increment" arising from this fortune Mr. Chamberlain is now living, the said increment coming into his pocket without putting him to the slightest exertion—other people doing all the work, he simply receiving the money.

From the height of this impregnable position he considers himself justified in calling the attention of the nation to the fact that Lord Salisbury is deriving an income without either toiling or spinning. He also considers himself justified in drawing attention to the fact that landowners are in possession of "unearned increment," an expression which, the *Times* remarks, he appears "to have got on the brain."

Let us see, if we can, what is the meaning of this "thoughtful" phraseology. So far as I understand it, reader, it means that if you or I purchase a piece of ground on which or near which people subsequently build houses or railways, or that from any other cause this ground becomes in process of time infinitely more valuable, the difference between the price we paid and the present value is "unearned increment," and as neither you nor I could have done anything in the way of toiling or spinning which would account for this increase in value, it should belong to the State and not to us. If, on the other hand, people should not build either houses or railways at or near our property, then the State should kindly allow us to keep our property and our loss.

On the other hand, if we were to invest our money in railways, say, at £50 per share, and (through no effort on our part) they become worth £150 per share, the difference in value would be our own, the distinction in the two cases being that the "unearned increment" in the former case would probably belong to a wicked Tory, and in the latter to a "thoughtful" Liberal.

Now, the gentleman who can draw these hair-splitting and imaginary distinctions between one class of property and another, and who can embody them in the cant phraseology of his party, for the purpose of manufacturing a handle for an attack upon property, and for impressing the masses with an idea that landowners are living upon what does not belong to them, is the same gentleman whose duty it is to see that the country is protected from the monopoly given by the State to Railway Companies. But so busy is he in straining at an imaginary "gnat," that he has apparently neither the time nor the will to take the slightest notice of the "camel," except by remarking "railways must know their own business best!" Probably a defiance of law, which results in a heavy tax upon land, is not without a certain charm to Mr.

Chamberlain's mind. The fact that bread stuffs can be conveyed from America to Londonderry at about half the cost that they can be sent from Londonderry to Co. Donegal, apparently proves to him the necessity of instituting further raids upon land and nothing more! The idea never seems to have struck him that, under these circumstances, *Irish land could not pay if it were rent free.*

It cannot be urged in excuse that he did not know the evidence, as it was his duty to know it. Besides this, the chairman of the committee was a Liberal, and a member of the Government; and Mr. Chamberlain must have known exactly how the report of the committee was arrived at, and that the verdict of "Not guilty" was (excepting the railway directors) only found by three members out of a total of twenty-seven. Yet we do not hear him explaining the nature of this farce to the masses, or informing them that it is the Railway Companies and not the landowners who are robbing the country. On the other hand, there is a strong suspicion that he intended the whole affair should be hushed up, and that Sir Thomas Farrer's manifesto was meant to allay any feeling of uneasiness on the public mind. Whether it was at his instigation that his Permanent Secretary wrote to the *Fortnightly Review*, it is impossible to say; but it is hardly probable that this gentleman would have been made a baronet except upon the recommendation of Mr. Chamberlain, and it is less likely that this would have been made had Sir Thomas taken so extraordinary a step without the knowledge and consent of his chief.

Turning to another subject, it is, of course, a well-known fact that there is no tyranny like the tyranny of the mob, and in order to prove to my readers that there is no despotism more pronounced or illogical than that administered by their leaders (after having attained power by bawling themselves hoarse for liberty and justice), I will relate the following little incident in Mr. Chamberlain's family history, which has been facetiously described by the press as the story of "Joseph and His Brethren."

It appears that Mr. Chamberlain has two brothers, who were candidates for election at the Reform Club. Now, it appears that these two young gentlemen were recently travelling in Australia, and (with the exception of their living after the manner of "the rich," and existing on the "unearned increment") their conduct in improving their minds by seeing the world appears to be not only unexceptionable but praiseworthy. However, it seems that some one at the Reform Club told some one else that something had or had not happened at the club at Melbourne (at which club the Messrs. Chamberlain had been honorary members) which, in his opinion, made it unfitting that these gentlemen should become members of the Reform, and the consequence of this conversation is believed to have resulted in their being blackballed. Now, as this operation merely signified that certain gentlemen declined their society, one would have imagined that there was no course open to them but to accept the decision; for if people do not want to associate with you, it seems not only difficult but inexpedient to try to compel them. However, this was not the view adopted by the Right Honourable Joseph Chamberlain, and he decided that if the members of the Reform Club did not wish to receive his brothers, they must be *compelled* to receive them; and he immediately took steps to effect this object. First of all, the law was set in motion against the member who had said the "something" referred to. Then all the members of the Government who could be obtained (including the Marquis of Hartington, and the Right Honourable John Bright) were brought down to the Reform Club by Mr. Chamberlain, for the purpose of altering the laws of that establishment. One would naturally suppose that his wish would be to alter them in the direction of giving individual members greater power of expressing their opinion; but this was by no means the case. The advocate for manhood suffrage and his friends came to propose that the franchise now enjoyed by the members should be taken away from them and invested in a committee, so that they should be prevented from deciding who they would or would not have as their associates. However, in spite of the powerful appeals of Lord Hartington and Mr. Bright, the Club refused to obey the Birmingham mandate, and the Messrs. Chamberlain have not yet been elected members of the Reform.

This incident forcibly illustrates the kind of freedom which will exist in England, if it ever happens that Mr. Chamberlain (with a manhood suffrage and paid Parliament) is allowed to exercise his "thoughtful" ingenuity on the property and liberty of the people of this country. That such a time will ever arrive, I do not believe, in spite of the fantastic legislation which for some years has been allowed to take place. Common sense is not yet quite extinct in England. The country will draw the line somewhere, and that somewhere will be very near Mr. Chamberlain. It is one thing for the country to swallow a poisonous pill gilded by such a master of the decorative art as Mr. Gladstone, but it does not follow that it will consent to receive a more deadly compound (in a singularly unattractive and nauseous form) from the leader of the Birmingham Caucus.

Mr. Chamberlain may characterize these remarks as coarse and vulgar, and I am willing to confess that allusion to the domestic history of politicians is not ordinarily a mark of good taste, but that gentleman must remember he has himself set the example. It is quite true that "two blacks do not make a white," but when a statesman uses politics for the purpose not only of setting class against class, but a class against an individual, it is excusable and indeed necessary to call the attention of "the people" to the fact that their would-be leader is no more of a purist in matters which touch his pocket and feelings than the most abandoned Tory in the land.

I cannot sum up this chapter on the "thoughtful" Liberal more fittingly than by quoting the descriptive remarks of a nobleman who formerly (before the advent of this political excrescence) was regarded as an advanced Liberal. I refer to the Duke of Argyll, and his words, in the House of Lords, on August 2, 1881, are these :—

> My lords, when I look at my noble friends below me on the treasury bench, I cannot help regarding them as something very like what I have seen on the shores of the western islands of Scotland—a row of jelly-fishes. My noble friends need not be affronted by the comparison. Jelly-fishes are the most beautiful creatures in the world. They have been studied by eminent biologists now for many years. It has been discovered that they are endowed with a most elaborate and delicate nervous system; but, I am sorry to say, they have hitherto been found destitute of a skeleton and a backbone. But there is one peculiarity about these jelly-fishes. They make the most beautiful convulsive movements in the water, and you see that the poor creatures think they are swimming; but when you take the bearings of the land, you find they are simply floating with the currents and the tides. That is the position of my noble friends with regard to this Irish Land Bill.

LAND.

FOR some reason or other the British Radical has always evinced the most violent antipathy to the landowning classes of this country. It is not at first sight easy to see the cause of this, except by recognizing the fact that extreme Radicalism is only thinly disguised Communism with restraining influences. These influences are comprised in the fact that the Radical himself possesses property, which he is no more wishful to relinquish than is the most ardent Conservative. If at one and the same time he could, somehow or other, keep possession of this property, and yet see Communism flourishing all around him, the dream of his life would be fulfilled; but at present even his "thoughtful" nature has been unable to formulate a theory compatible with this state of things.

In land, however, he sees a species of property which he can attack in the direction of his ideal without at all interfering with his goods and chattels, and in doing so he has an opportunity of expressing his sympathy with the distressed agriculturist, and showing him how thoroughly the farmers' interests are bound up with the Radical policy. "Land," he solemnly assures us, "belongs to the people;" and there we all agree with him to this extent, viz. "that the things in the world belong to the world," but in no other sense. People have bought and sold land, and exercised the rights of property over it from time immemorial, just in the same way as they have dealt in anything else. "But," says the Radical, "times are altered. Land in the United Kingdom is limited; the people are constantly increasing, and must be fed," etc. The "thoughtful" one forgets, however, that all this has been going on for hundreds of years. The land of this country has long ceased to support the population, and what food we require we buy from other countries, just as they buy coal, iron, and other articles they want from us. Nothing shows how completely independent the people are of British grown corn than the fact that during the last seven or eight years of deficient harvests, and in spite of the increased population, bread stuffs were never so cheap. The various products of land are bought and sold and subjected to the like law of supply and demand as any other article of trade, and it requires a considerable stretch of imagination to see how the grower, who has the most perfect freedom of action with regard to his produce, should be artificially protected in his possession of the land which gives him that produce. It amounts to the same thing as if a man had invested money, say, in a cloth mill and fitted it with machinery, and were to let it to another person upon certain terms; and that after the bargain was made and the lessee had commenced to make cloth, the law were to step in and say to the owner of the mill, "The terms you have made with your tenant are not sufficiently liberal. You must allow him to remain on quite different terms, or you must pay him a large sum for going out."

It would be just as reasonable or as rational to go to the tenant and say to him, "The people you sell to are very poor, but it is necessary they should be clothed. You charge a high price for the clothes you make. We will alter all contracts you have entered into for the sale of your clothes."

Interference of this kind is perfectly absurd and illogical, looked at from any possible point of view.

However, let us for the moment accept the proposition and allow that the land belongs to the people. What does the Radical propose to do? Does he suggest that it should be cut up into so many square yards and divided in equal quantities amongst the population? If so, I am content to leave the suggestion unanswered, and dedicate it to the thoughtful reflection of my readers. If not, there remains the necessity that land must be held by the Government or the ordinary landowner. Does the Radical imagine that it would pay the people of this country for them to borrow, through the Government, money at three per cent., and expend that money in buying land which, taken over the whole United Kingdom, would probably not return them one and a half per cent.?

Would it pay the farmer to have his rent collected, whether the seasons were bad or good, in the same way as his taxes are called for? Would it answer his purpose to have no landlord to whom he could go in a bad season and ask for time, and probably also obtain an important reduction in rent? I trow not!

As it would pay neither of the parties I have referred to, the question naturally arises, How is it that landlords are contented to receive a return for their money so small that it would satisfy no other section of the community? The answer is, that the land in this country possesses two separate values—the one is a commercial value, which varies with the productive powers of the land; the other is a sentimental value. Land gives, or is supposed to give (especially when possessed in large quantities), a certain prestige to the owner, and for that prestige rich men are prepared to pay; that is, they are prepared to buy land and let the farmer have the use of it at so low a rental as to make it impossible for the ordinary investor to regard it for a moment in the light of a paying investment. This, surely, is a great advantage to the farmer and to the country at large. It really gives a value of untold millions to property in these islands, and though that value may be a sentimental one, it is, nevertheless, perfectly real when property comes into the market, viz. that an estate, when thrown upon the market, produces so many thousands more than its intrinsic value entitles it to, and it is precisely of this value that the Radical, by his pernicious meddling, is constantly striving to deprive it. The Hares and Rabbits' Bill went a considerable way in this direction, and also levelled a direct blow at freedom of contract. A man who owns a landed estate may, if so disposed, turn the whole thing into a game farm, obtaining also what crops he can. Another man may be able to see his way to take the estate at so low a rental that it will pay him to farm it in spite of the game. The landlord may be willing almost to give him the use of the farm, to save himself from the trouble of farming; and yet our sapient legislators have decided that these parties are not to have the power of making a mutually advantageous contract, as the farmer cannot divest himself of the right of killing every hare and rabbit in the place.

Radicals are never tired of discoursing on the evils of absentee landlordism in Ireland, whilst doing their best to make the system general in England. If, however, absenteeism is prejudicial to one country, it follows that it must be prejudicial to the other. In England there are thousands of properties on which the landlords cannot afford to live, but there are also a great number of capitalists who are always willing to take their houses and shooting, and in this way disburse in the neighbourhood the money which under different circumstances would be spent by the landlords. The law has now stepped in and said to the capitalist, "You shall not take houses and shooting in England, or, if you do, when you go out shooting any farmer may range the fields in front of you, for the purpose of killing hares and rabbits." The money loss to the country from houses and shooting unlet on account of the Hares and Rabbits' Bill can hardly be over-estimated. The landlord loses the rent; the farmer loses all the incidental advantages connected with the fact of a rich man being upon the property; and the labourer loses endless small comforts and assistance in times of distress. It means the entire difference of a great house being kept up and some thousands a year spent in the immediate neighbourhood, or its being left to go to decay, and, to a great extent, the neighbourhood with it. In fact, the whole evils of absentee landlordism are involved.

Farmers were, as a rule, quite able to take care of themselves and did not require any coddling from Radicals, so far as bargains were concerned. If a landlord kept an undue quantity of game, it may be taken for granted that the farmer was paid for it in some way or another. If not, the latter simply made a foolish bargain, and will, in spite of any number of remedial measures, probably make more. No law can protect a foolish man from making bad bargains. As a matter of fact, however, farms in heavy game-preserving countries were sought after just as eagerly as any others, and it is therefore reasonable to presume that the farmer received a *quid pro quo*.

The Agricultural Holdings Bill is the advanced guard of another Radical attack on land, and may be looked upon as occupying a similar position towards land in England as the Irish Land Bill of 1870 did to land in Ireland, and will probably require about the same amount of amending. No sooner is the Bill passed than the advanced Radical is clamouring for more. The Bill is simply one for giving to tenants that which they never contracted for when they made their agreements. All that it gives (if it is worth anything) amounts to a direct taking away from the landlords. To be logical, if it is to have any effect in the long run, Government must fix judicial rents, as in Ireland, because it stands to reason that any value given to the tenant beyond that included in his original contract with his landlord can be discounted and charged for in the rent. The farm which was worth so much before the increased value given to it by the legislature is worth so much more afterwards, and exactly that sum can be put on the rent for the future.

A Scotch farmer (farming on a most extensive scale, and paying some £6000 a year in rent) was recently asked his opinion on this Bill, and he replied that "It will be a good thing for the lawyers;" and this it will assuredly prove. Neither land nor farming have paid very well recently; and the Government, by way of helping them, have introduced what will amount to a direct and certainly unproductive tax, which will have to be borne between the landlord and tenant in the shape of law charges, whenever any question arises which will involve the adaptation of the new law to contracts made on the faith of the old one. Any one who has experience of these matters will be able to judge whether these are likely to be heavy or light. The great principle at the bottom of this legislation seems to be, that if certain classes are not doing well, the law should step in and make their bargains, leaving them to deal with the costs.

There is, however, something much worse than any of the evils I have mentioned, which is the direct consequence of these attacks upon land. I refer to the fact that *no one will buy it!* My readers must have constantly heard the remark made by people to the effect that nothing would induce them to buy land, as " no one knows, from moment to moment, what the Government will do next."

There are thousands of poor landlords in England who can neither assist nor relieve the farmer in his extremities ; and there are thousands of capitalists who would be most willing to take advantage of the present low values to invest in land, and who would and could tide the farmer over his difficulties, but they are prevented from doing so by the fatuous conduct of the Government. How can any man in his senses (who reflects upon what has taken place in Ireland, and sees the thin end of the wedge applied to this kingdom) be expected to invest money in a property of which he is nearly certain to be wholly or partially deprived, if the present Government remains in office any length of time? Who in his senses can be expected to invest in property in which, when it is let on perfectly legal terms, the Government of the day claims the right to step in and make different terms.

These are the reasons which compel the needy landowner, with his heavily mortgaged estate, to remain as he is, doing no good to himself or his farmers.

These are the causes which prevent the capitalist from coming to the rescue, and which compel him to let his money lie idle, or remain invested in other countries, whilst it is so urgently needed in England. It is no exaggeration to say that the conduct of the Radicals, in giving expression to their unreasoning hatred of the landowners, has depreciated the value of property in this country to the extent of hundreds of millions. This, it must be remembered, does not only affect land, but directly or indirectly every class and every species of property in this country; that is to say, the nation at large is so much poorer from the want of confidence engendered. This lack of confidence is the direct result of Governmental interference in matters beyond its province, and forms one of the most crushing burdens a country can be called upon to bear.

IRISH LAND ACTS.

ALTHOUGH the Irish Land Act of 1870, compared with recent legislation, may be looked upon as a venial measure, it created some little astonishment on its introduction. For the first time it was observed that, on the ground of expediency, the Radicals were prepared to break with the old political economy of which the Liberals of former days had been the most determined exponents. But the astonishment gave way to a feeling of confidence when people listened to or read the glowing words of Mr. Gladstone on the introduction of the measure, and heard how his proposed "messages of peace" would not only bring contentment and good will to Ireland and restore prosperity to that unhappy country, but at the same time would solve a very awkward political problem, upon which the minds of successive Governments had so long been exercised. What chance had the hard dry facts of political economy against his impassioned and sympathetic oratory, when explaining to an entranced House of Commons and to the people of this country all the blessings which would flow from their abandonment?

The Bill was passed, and, as my readers are aware, the result was not altogether assuring!

The only feelings of gratitude perceptible on the minds of the Irish people seemed to be comprised "in a lively anticipation of favours to come," and subsequent Radical legislation has shown they were not mistaken in their diagnosis of the situation.

The Conservatives came into power in 1874, and had to deal with the state of expectancy into which the Irish nation had been plunged. The events which occurred compelled them to pass a Bill, called the Peace Preservation Act, which operated so beneficially that Mr. Gladstone, in his celebrated Midlothian campaign, characterized the state of Ireland as being more peaceful than it had been for many years previously. But this, reader, was not intended as a compliment to the Conservative Government, but as a reason why the clamour of the dissatisfied classes in Ireland, for the repeal of the above-mentioned Act, should be complied with. It must be remembered that at this time even the most enthusiastic Liberal never thought it probable that they would obtain a majority at the ensuing election. Their great hope was that by reducing the Conservative ranks, and by obtaining for their own side the united support of the Irish party, the Conservative administration would be so weakened as to be practically unworkable.

I mention this for the purpose of showing that when Mr. Gladstone made the remarks I have alluded to, and others to which I shall shortly have to refer, he was a "free lance," with no sense of responsibility, and undeterred by those patriotic sentiments which have hitherto been supposed to restrain our statesmen from making party capital out of questions involving the disintegration of this kingdom. But there was more to come! The present Prime Minister informed his hearers that even the very crimes (the like of which the Peace Preservation Act had been passed to prevent) were not without redeeming features! He proceeded to explain to them that the murder of an English policeman engaged in the ordinary duty of his office, and the attempted blowing up of an extensive prison in which hundreds of persons narrowly escaped death (and for which acts the miserable perpetrators had either been hanged or sent to penal servitude), had not been without use, and, in fact, had done a great great deal for Ireland. He explained that these dreadful crimes had made possible in politics what had been impossible before. That, whereas, previously to their commission, such great measures as the Disestablishment of the Church and the Irish Land Act had not been "within the range of practical politics," yet afterwards they were not only practical, but had been enacted, and were at that moment part of the law of the country. Now, as before-mentioned, he was not in office, and had no reasonable expectation of occupying it. In fact, from hints thrown out by the right honourable gentleman himself, after his defeat in 1874, people were under the impression that his future leisure was to be employed in those wholesome reflections which are believed to bring so much comfort to the declining period of life.

But the irony of fate willed it otherwise. The Liberals unexpectedly returned to power, and Mr. Gladstone then decided to defer his reflective period to a more convenient opportunity, and to once again hold the reins of office. He it was, therefore, and not the Conservative leader, who had to reckon with the effect of his Midlothian utterances on the minds of the Irish people; and my readers may imagine the task was no light one. The people most unmistakably showed that they were preparing to bring more matters within political range by the use of the old well-tried machinery. It was therefore necessary that something more should be done, and done quickly; and, in order to waste no time, the Chief Secretary for Ireland made a declaration of the Government policy. He stated that the Government's idea of administration in Ireland was "to govern it according to Irish ideas;" and as "Irish ideas" seemed to include the right of shooting landlords, this policy seemed sufficiently comprehensive to cover everything the Irish could possibly want. But in order to accentuate this statement, and leave no possible doubt on the mind of the most incredulous Irishman, he proceeded to point out the means to be adopted, viz. that the Government would do exactly the opposite to what the Conservatives had done. With these two fundamental principles in view, they commenced operations, and naturally the first work was to abolish the Peace Preservation Act. This, of course, cleared the way for the people to make considerably larger use of the "practical politics" machinery, which they were not slow to avail themselves of. Murder and outrage occurred with monotonous regularity, and very soon produced an effect on the mind of the Prime Minister similar to that to which he had alluded at Midlothian.

A brand-new Irish Land Act was the result; and it was a Bill which not only dwarfed its predecessor, but showed unmistakably that the last rag of adhesion to the old economic laws was to be ruthlessly torn away, and sacrificed at the altar of Radical expediency. The Act also possessed the advantage of giving the advanced section of the Radicals just a "taste of blood." Land, as previously mentioned, had long been singled out for attack, and this was an opportunity for whetting the Radical appetite, without directly appearing to do so, all being included in the so-called "remedial measures for Ireland." However, Parliament, forgetful of the experience of 1870, passed the Bill, and commissioners were at once appointed to scamper all over the country, and go through the farce of fixing so-called "judicial rents;" but it was merely a clumsy and costly method of taking a certain amount of money from the loyal and law-abiding classes, and giving it to the disloyal and law-breakers.

This Act had been preceded by the Compensation for Disturbance Bill, which was thrown out by the House of Lords, and was followed by the Arrears Bill, which simply amounted to a premium on dishonesty. It meant a good deal for people who had not paid their rents, and nothing for those who had. The Radical departures not only provided for the banishing of economic laws to other planets, but also for the expulsion of morality at the same time.

In spite of all this desperate legislation, the machinery for the production of more was never allowed to remain idle in Ireland, and the Government never appeared to make any great effort to stop it, except by the production of the measures referred to, which had the same effect as oil thrown upon flames.

The difficulty of the Government was great. They could not well reintroduce the Peace

Preservation Act, for that would hardly amount to doing "exactly the opposite to what the Conservatives had done," and, besides which, at this time an eminent member of the Cabinet made the singular discovery that "force was no remedy." This seemed to prove conclusively to the Government that there was only one course open. Remedial measures were of no use, force was no remedy, and the only thing left was a submission to the inevitable. That is to say, the Irish landlord, after being judicially robbed, was left to his own resources to avoid being extra-judicially murdered.

And so things went on until the Chief Secretary, in spite of the recent discovery of the Cabinet minister alluded to (and in spite of its having been effectually used by Conservatives), was at length rash enough to suggest the use of force. No one outside the precincts of the Cabinet quite knew what happened when this astounding suggestion was made, but everybody knew that the erring Chief Secretary did not long afterwards remain a member of the Government, and his retirement led to the unfortunate appointment of Lord Frederick Cavendish, who, together with his

R

secretary, Mr. Burke, was murdered on the first day of his arrival in the country. This appalling crime had the effect of awakening the Government from the state of stupor into which it had fallen, and from which the long list of previous murders and atrocities had been insufficient to arouse it. Then, and then only, did it become evident that force was not only a remedy but *the* remedy. To supply this, the Crimes Act was passed—an Act which, in its Draconian enactments, far outstripped any measures the Conservatives had found it necessary to adopt, in order to bring about that state of "profound peace" alluded to by Mr. Gladstone at Midlothian. The Act has, however, proved eminently successful; and it is now perfectly clear that the lives previously lost —lives equally as valuable to their friends and relatives as either Lord Frederick Cavendish's or Mr. Burke's were to theirs—were sacrificed by the supineness of the Government, engendered not only by the Quixotic notions of certain members of the Cabinet, but by a lack of worldly wisdom and want of knowledge of human nature, which extended over the whole body to an almost inconceivable degree. The Irish Invincibles,

Irish Land Acts.

although balked in Ireland, did not forget that it was to crime in England to which the Midlothian utterances referred, and that the latter country was still open to them. They produced at the Government offices an almost exact counterpart to the Clerkenwell explosion, and, had not the police frustrated their efforts, were preparing a scheme for the foundation of "practical politics" on so vast a scale that a considerable portion of London seemed doomed to destruction. Shortly after the explosion referred to, several of the daily papers inserted extracts from the speech of Mr. O'Donnell, M.P., and also an extract from the *Daily Express*, both of which I give as under:—

"Mr. O'Donnell, M.P., speaking last night at an Irish Meeting at Sheffield, alluded to the explosion in London, and said that the great and holy cause of Ireland could not be benefited by outrage or by crime which openly offered excuses to the advocates of tyranny and coercion. Mr. Gladstone had himself said that such dreadful events as the explosion of Clerkenwell did more to bring the Irish question within the arena of practical politics than all the arguments of Butts and O'Connell. But he denied it. Though foolish English statesmen might give vent to utterances of that description, which were calculated to encourage outrage and crime, he maintained that the cause of Ireland would be supported and carried to a triumphant end by the calm reply and law-abiding determination of an united and patriotic people."

The Irish *Daily Express* says, " While all eyes are angrily turned upon the Irish party, the person whom we believe to be chiefly responsible for these and such like outrages escapes. The whole political career of Mr. Gladstone has been one standing argument to the Irish democrats, that if they would bend him to their purpose they must have recourse to some such tactics. Mr. Gladstone's declaration that the Clerkenwell explosion brought the land question and the Church question within a measurable distance of practical politics has been ever since the charter and justification of all such ruffianism. He has taught, not only by his words but by his acts, that if the extreme Irish party desire his assistance in carrying out their revolutionary designs they must seek it by assassination, outrage, and diabolical wickedness. When this wickedness has reached some superlative and theatrical point, then he steps into the arena and strikes with his legislative weapons on the same side. This is the lesson he has taught his Irish pupils, and they have not been slow to profit by it. Thus Mr. Gladstone has done more to foster and cherish Irish Nihilism than any promoter of disorder with whom we are acquainted, not excepting Mr. Parnell or the editor of the *Irish World*."

If my readers, after perusing these statements, can come to the conclusion that the strictures on the Prime Minister contained in them were entirely undeserved, I am sure they will do so with a profound sigh of relief. Referring, however, again to the period in which the "force no remedy" principle prevailed in the Cabinet, it was curious to observe that the houses of Cabinet ministers were guarded night and day by stalwart policemen, and also that the owners never ventured out without being followed by detectives. But it was more curious still to try to imagine what the feelings of those members of Parliament could be who had helped Mr. Gladstone to bring in his Irish measures dating from 1870, and who remembered how, under the witchery and glamour of his unequalled eloquence, they had surrendered those fundamental rules and principles which had hitherto governed not only their proceedings, but those of every civilized Government in the world. Those who remembered how, under the plea of "exceptional circumstances," they had been induced by comforting promises and assurances to surrender their own common-sense and place themselves body and soul in his hands, had now an opportunity of observing that the effects of all his fine words had culminated in the fact that the country was compelled to pay policemen for the special purpose of protecting the lives of the members of its Government.

Yet our "thoughtful" Radical has learnt nothing from all this! He is still looking forward with fervent hopes to similar legislative triumphs.

Already we hear that the Crimes Act has done its work and can be repealed. We are also informed by a member of the Government, closely related to the Prime Minister, that the Land Bill already requires amendment; but whether this statement is the effect of a conception of his own perceptive intellect, coupled to an alarming extent with the "courage of his opinions," or whether he is merely used as a feather thrown up to show the way of the wind, it is impossible to say; for in this extraordinary Cabinet it is the custom for individual members to air their respective theories, quite independently of the expressed opinion of the Cabinet as a whole. There is, however, a considerable amount of method in this apparent madness; for whilst the different sections of Radicals and the extreme Irish party are played to by individual members, the Government as a whole mildly deprecate the extreme utterances of their members, and in this way the fears of their Whig supporters are assuaged. Looked at from any possible point of view, the Government policy in Ireland, with the exception of that which occurred subsequently to the murder of Lord Frederick Cavendish, has been one series of fatal blunders. The prevailing idea on the mind of the Government seems to have been that it was possible and feasible to restore law and order from a state of the utmost anarchy, by passing Bills giving other people's money to the law-breakers. Any more direct incentive to further outrage (taken in connection with Mr. Gladstone's words) cannot be conceived, and of this the Government were fully warned, both by the press and in the House of Commons. The *St. James's Gazette*, in writing of the Land Bill of 1880, compared it to "giving a tiger a bite of your leg, and hoping it would be satisfied;" and this, in so many words, aptly described the situation.

However, the Government not only had a majority, but a majority largely composed of the "earnest and thoughtful" type who were burning to signalize their return to power by legislative fireworks of the most novel description, and, in spite of all warnings, this majority they were determined to use.

But, readers, there are certain laws working under the surface of things, which after violation are sure sooner or later to reassert themselves, and cover with confusion their shortsighted opponents, equally whether they be termed Communists or Cabinet ministers. In this case, the Government has elucidated no new principle showing how the future Irish tenant is to live, or even how his position is to be ameliorated; but, on the other hand, it has made it infinitely worse. Money has been taken from Brown the landlord and given to Jones the tenant. But let us see what happens when Jones dies or gives up his farm, and Smith wants to take his place. Let us see whether Smith will have much reason to bless this "remedial legislation." His position will be this: Jones (or Jones's representative) will ask him in the first place to pay the ordinary tenant right, and will then ask him to pay a sum of money equal to the annual sum capitalized, which the Government took from Brown and gave to Jones. Smith, in order to raise sufficient to pay both the charges, will probably have to apply to the Gombeen man, who will advance it at a sufficiently high rate of interest to pay him for the risk incurred. Thus to Smith's judicial rent will have to be added the interest paid on capital taken from the landlord and given to the late tenant, which will amount to far more than the original rent, because the money-lender will have to make his profit out of the transaction; and in bad times the wretched Smith will have this proverbial gentleman to deal with, instead of a considerate landlord; so that the Government, by way of helping the husbandry of the future in Ireland, have introduced two entirely new and unproductive taxes, viz. the lawyer and the money-lender, for which the Irish nation has about the same cause for thankfulness as the Israelites had for the legislation of Pharoah. On the other hand, the United Kingdom has not much greater cause for joy; for, anomalous as it may appear, it has had to pay in increased taxation nearly the full sum the tenants have received from their landlords, as the cumbersome machinery appointed by the Government has absolutely swallowed up in expenses nearly as much money as the Land Commissioners have given to the tenants; so that it works out in this way, viz.: 1st. That the landlords have been robbed for the sole benefit of the tenant in possession, and to the injury of the next one. 2nd. That in future the lawyer and the money-lender will batten upon both landlord and tenant. 3rd. That the whole country will be called upon to pay for the costly machinery necessary to produce these happy effects. 4th. That by the destruction of confidence, a most deadly blow has been struck at the prosperity of Ireland; for clearly no capitalist will come to the assistance of either landlord or tenant, obvious as it must be to the meanest capacity that a Government which takes four shillings in the pound to-day may take the remaining sixteen to-morrow.

But there is yet another feature connected with Irish land legislation, viz. that the English Government seized upon private property for the purpose of defraying the expenses of an object which (whether right or wrong) was a purely national one, and, as such, should have been paid out of the national exchequer. This, to a civilized community, is an indelible disgrace; and in this case not diminished by the remembrance of the fact that the family of the minister who inaugurated the crusade had within comparatively recent years been heavily compensated (and properly so) for the enforced emancipation of slaves which they possessed. Surely the possession of land in Ireland was as right, as just, or as laudable as the possession of slaves in the West Indies; and every argument used by the Prime Minister in the House of Commons on the iniquity and injustice of emancipating the slaves without compensating the owners, could have been used with equal or greater force in respect to the confiscation of land or land's worth. But *tempora mutantur!* The Prime Minister was aware that if he boldly proposed to the British taxpayer that he should hand over so much money to the law-breakers in Ireland, he would have been hurled from office, and therefore he adopted the more prudent course of singling out a rather isolated and comparatively defenceless class of the community, and compelling them to find the money for the disastrous legislation I have enlarged upon.

CLASS LEGISLATION.

THE great principle underlying all recent or projected legislation is a continuous effort to make laws in the interests of or against particular classes, quite irrespective of the fact that the interests of all sections of society are bound together indissolubly, and an injury to one is an injury to all.

The chief characteristic of Liberalism in years gone by was the absolute freedom advocated in buying, selling, and in making of contracts. Liberals of those days recognized the fact that the art of good government in matters of this kind consisted in leaving people alone ; but those politicians have, unfortunately, been succeeded by a kind of political prig who affects to understand the business of other people a great deal better than they understand it themselves, and instead of the liberty formerly enjoyed, there is nothing now but a continual repetition of "you shall do this," and "you shall not do that," according to the whim of the particular doctrinaire in power, and the country as a whole suffers in exact proportion. To illustrate my meaning, I will quote a few extracts from a letter of a learned judge, who, for a knowledge of law and strong common sense (attributes not always combined), has probably no equal. I refer to Lord Bramwell, and the letter was read at a meeting of the Liberty and Property Defence League. He says—

"My opinions of half a century standing are as strong as ever. I like to be governed as little as possible, and what I like for myself I like for others. No one knows my wants as well as myself, and I am pretty sure no one will take so much pains as I do to gratify them. I am certain it is best to leave what I may call natural causes to operate and bring about natural results. I cannot but think our present troubles show this."

Lord Penzance, in a letter to the same society, says—

"Since the gross departure from all principle has set the example in Ireland of fixing rents by law, numerous classes are beginning to turn their eyes to the legislature to improve their position, and the sooner a firm stand is made in the assertion of those principles of free dealing between man and man, which were once the watchword of the Liberal party, the better it will be for all classes."

But the difference between the Liberalism of the past and the Liberalism of the present is perhaps even more graphically described at the same meeting by Mr. Pochin, a prominent Liberal, for, after describing the hundreds of speeches he has heard under the banner of "Buy in the cheapest market and sell in the dearest," he is reported to have said—

"They had been told by Messrs. Cobden and Bright that they were to view with the greatest jealousy any legislation that interfered with that wholesome rule of commercial enterprise. If such legislation were attempted, they were to protest without ceasing against it. They were met to-day for the purpose of protesting, and were going to protest without ceasing against legislation that warred so entirely as did the Irish Land Act against that very wholesome and, they believed, sound doctrine. A gentleman, having a name second only to Mr. Bright himself in the corn law agitation, had said to him (Mr. Pochin) recently, 'If you establish a court in Dublin to settle the amount of rent a tenant should pay to his landlord, I defy you logically to abstain from establishing a court in London to settle the amount of wages the employer should pay to the employed;' and he asked if the meeting was prepared for such legislation. If they were not, it was high time that a vigorous protest should be heard throughout the length and breadth of the land. It was to him a matter of great pain that Mr. Bright should so far forget the doctrines which he was at one time ever ready to teach and preach, for the short-sighted purpose that he might in the most easy way overcome the difficulties that at the moment beset the Cabinet.

"One word about Mr. Gladstone. He had been a member of the Political Economy Club for some seventeen years. That club had been composed of the most eminent thinkers of the day, and Mr. Gladstone had often and often listened to their discussions. It was more than startling, it was grievous, to find him saying now that you might legislate in accordance with the doctrines of political economy for the planets of Saturn and Jupiter, but that such legislation would not do for this country. In his (Mr. Pochin's) view of the matter, the doctrines of political economy, so far as they were established, meant acting on those principles that would give to the inhabitants of a country or district the largest supply of the necessities and comforts of life. It was, in fact, the great doctrine of economics, and as well might Mr. Gladstone say that it was all very well to legislate for Saturn and Jupiter, as if two and two made four, but that such a principle could not be acted upon in legislating for this country. He had in the past thoroughly believed in Messrs. Gladstone and Bright. He had at the last election given a large portion of time and money, and all the votes he could command, to place his former political friend in office. He now felt that their proceedings were so far removed from their past teachings, that it was impossible his voice could be raised in their favour, until they had returned to those principles that were ever true, and of which in the past they had been the most eloquent and the most able advocates."

Ever since freedom of contract and the truths

of political economy were thus openly and ostentatiously declared obsolete, it follows that Radical legislation has amounted to a mere drifting, simply to a floating with the stream without chart or compass, and leading no one knows whither.

Acts of Parliament founded on no fixed principle invariably fail to attain the object for which they are passed, and the Radical in boldly declaring for their amendment is never in the least abashed by the falsification of all his promises on their introduction.

It is only a few years since the Ballot Act was introduced, with the full brass band accompaniment of Radical music. Its advocates prophesied a glorious revolution in English politics. There would be no more corruption, no more undue influence; voters would walk to the poll free men and incorruptible, and blessings untold would follow in the usual course. Ten years later, Lord Granville refers to the sorrowful sequel. His lordship, in addressing a meeting of delegates from Liberal Associations (with reference to the election of 1880, which placed the Liberal party in power), said—

"I believe there is no doubt that a greater

number of individuals were bribed than had ever been bribed before."

This was said for the purpose of proving the necessity of the Corrupt Practices Act, the inevitable amendment to a great Radical measure!

In reference to this Act, it has been stated, and I believe with some truth, that a candidate's chance of getting into prison has, by its provisions, been made considerably greater than his chance of getting into Parliament.

In any case, it has laid the foundation for endless petitions, waste of judicial time, enormous law expenses, and years of the utmost ill-feeling amongst the inhabitants of the towns in which these petitions are tried. The originator of the Act appears to have ignored the legal maxim, "*De minimis non curat lex;*" for many of its provisions are petty and ridiculous to the last degree, giving the whole measure the appearance of a kind of legislative mouse-trap.

The Government who introduced it with apparently such devout horror of bribery is presided over by the same minister, who, previous to the general election of 1874, finding himself losing seat after seat, went to the country with a cry of "No Income Tax."

Everything else having failed, he resolved to try the effect of a direct appeal to the pockets of the constituencies; but the country, perceiving the hollowness of the offer, refused to be cajoled, and subequent events have fully justified its decision; for although Mr. Gladstone has been in office since 1880, he has not (as you and I, reader, are fully aware) redeemed his promises, nor does he hold out the slightest hope of doing anything of the kind.

Since the Liberal party returned to power, they have inaugurated one vast system of bribery—not with their own, but with the money of others—and this is exemplified nowhere more unblushingly than in their Irish legislation, and is none the less real because hidden beneath a cloak of virtuous sentiment and fine language. Under the assumption of self-sacrificing virtue and soaring patriotism, the Radical does nothing but offer, directly or indirectly, the property of the classes who have few votes to the classes who have many. No industry or property is safe, and in the general effect upon the country we are now realizing the truth of the

Class Legislation.

Scriptural adage, that "A house divided against itself cannot stand."

In addition to all this, there is a system of bureaucracy springing up amongst us, which, whilst entailing enormous expenditure of public money, materially assists the Government in rewarding the services of their thick and thin supporters.

The Earl of Derby, in a letter to the State Resistance Union, says—

"To resist *all* extension of State interference would be useless and probably mischievous, but I agree with your friends in holding that the modern tendency to increased state control in every department of life is one which requires to be watched with the utmost care, tending as it does to jobbery, to needless public expenditure, and to the undue restrictions of individual freedom."

With the introduction of the caucus, however, our taxes from the above-mentioned cause bid fair to assume colossal proportions. In the recent appointment of bankruptcy receivers, how many "earnest and thoughtful" Liberals seem to have been provided with modest independencies at the expense of the country!

As usual (and this time almost before the Radical introductory trumpet notes have died away), it begins to be whispered that the Act is a gigantic failure, and that the only appreciable and lasting effect will be that the above-mentioned gentlemen are simply provided with sinecures for life. At least, this seems to be the opinion of a gentleman who has had some experience in these matters. I refer to Mr. J. Russell, secretary to the late Mercantile Law Amendment Society, who, in a letter to the *Standard*, after pointing out the ruinous expenses of the new Act, says—

"In fact, black mail is levied all round, and creditors will find they have merely exchanged one set of wreckers for another equally rapacious, and it may be safely presumed that in less than twelve months the new law will be as universally condemned as any of its predecessors. What, then, is to happen? From all I can learn, creditors, where a debtor has an estate, will go back to the old system of deeds of assignment; and where there are no assets, they will not interfere. We shall, therefore, practically be without any bankruptcy law at all. The President of the Board of Trade has, in all these matters, had his own way. He has had and exercised uncontrolled authority in framing the bankruptcy rules and fees. How these functions have been performed, I have enabled the public to judge. He has also created an enormous staff of officials at a very great cost to the country, and he has done his best to make their offices sinecures by driving all bankruptcy suitors from the courts."

Mr. Chamberlain's Fishing-boats Act seems to be preparing the way for more official patronage of a similar kind. This measure is referred to by Lord Bramwell in the following words :—

"The outcry against the Fishing-boats Act almost reconciles me to its passing, for it has shown to a stout and energetic body of men the folly and mischief of such interference with individual liberty. I think, however, any decent man might be afraid to be a skipper or to take an apprentice since this Act, which bristles with penalties and new offences. A lawyer should be one of every crew."

What with land commissioners in Ireland, and inspectors and receivers of every sort and kind springing up on all sides in England, if this legislation is to continue in its progressive rate, we may look forward to the time when one half of the population will be paid to watch or control the other half.

Another marked feature of our Radical Government is the importance attached by it to the opinions of any small band of agitators who, by holding public meetings or other means, succeed in bringing their views into prominence. Our statesmen appear to forget that, whilst in any large town or centre there are always a sufficient number of half-crazy individuals to get up an enthusiastic meeting on any conceivable subject, yet, for every person who attends such meetings, there are probably hundreds who not only do not attend, but who disagree entirely with the object for which they are called. The Government, however, persist in recognizing in gatherings of this kind the voice of the country. Even anti-vaccinationists have been assured by Mr. Gladstone that "his mind is open." Mr. Bright goes to the extent of declaring that if these people choose to pay a fine of a few shillings on one occasion, it is a monstrous injustice that they should not ever afterwards be allowed the right to decimate population by the spread of small-pox.

There is also another small band of eccentrics,

aptly described by a member of Parliament as consisting of "masculine women and effeminate men," who have succeeded, by persistent importunity, in obtaining the withdrawal of the grant for the carrying out of the Contagious Diseases Act, and never possibly was the effect of yielding to unreasoning clamour more appallingly or instantaneously shown. In reference to this subject, the *Lancet* states that at the annual meeting of the Royal Albert Hospital, at Devonport, all the speakers testified to the disastrous effect of the suspension of the Acts.

Archdeacon Earle said—

"The number of juveniles leading an evil course he saw in the streets, contrasted greatly with a year ago. Rescue and prevention are much less frequent, while open profligacy has become rampant, and the condition of the streets is relapsing into the disgusting state which preceded the passing of the Acts."

It was stated that the average number of cases of disease contracted among the military in the district during the five years on the old system was 30·87 per 1000; whilst in the first quarter of the voluntary system the ratio had risen to 102·5, and the statistics of the Naval Hospital at Stonehouse were still more frightful.

Now, putting on one side the effect on the health of the population generally, can any more desperate act, on the part of a Government, be conceived than that, for the purpose of stopping the noisy clamour of a handful of silly people, they should have allowed disease to increase among our soldiers to the extent of seventy men in every thousand, and this in the incredibly short period of three months. Even looking at the matter in its lowest form, that of expediency, is our army in such a state that we can spare these men from active service, or should the taxpayer be called upon to pay for them, when for all practical purposes they have ceased to exist? When it is remembered that this question affects the health, not only of the present generation, but of thousands of unborn innocents in succeeding ones, and that the suspension of the Acts really means sentences of disease and death distributed broadcast throughout the land, one cannot view this crowning act of our effete Government with feelings other than that of absolute nausea.

In the present session we are threatened with

legislation from another band of enthusiasts, termed Local Optionists. These people have a precedent for fairly claiming the assistance of the Government in embodying their particular craze in an Act of Parliament, and will probably receive it.

Their main idea is to give a certain majority of ratepayers in any district powers to suppress all public-houses within that district, and this would not only amount to a direct and tyrannical interference with the liberty of the subject, but would levy another severe blow at trade, and instead of furthering the cause of temperance, would have a distinctly opposite effect. If such a Bill were passed, it would mean—

1st. That the working classes would at once commence to brew their own beer, as they were formerly accustomed to do.

2nd. That the country would in this way lose the excise duty on this beer, and the amount would have to be made up in increased taxation.

3rd. That unless the owners of the public-houses so suppressed were fully compensated for the loss of their business, it would be nothing less than a gigantic State robbery.

4th. That if so compensated, the British taxpayer would be called upon to pay a considerably larger sum than he has any idea of.

5th. That the workmen would club together to buy spirituous liquor in small casks or convenient quantities (with which tradesmen will be always ready to supply them); that the liquors will be consumed in private houses, in company with the women and children; that these private houses will, for a purpose, become public-houses of the very worst kind, without any check to drunkenness, open all Sundays, or to any hour of the night; and that by this means intemperance will be largely increased.

I will now give an illustration from my own practical experience of what would happen.

In some extensive works in which I am a shareholder, on their opening, the directors decided to allow no public-house, and for some years there was none, the result being that the village became one of the most drunken and disorderly ones in the country. Exactly what I have described took place—one of every few houses being turned into a private drinking-shop, with the result that the women became as intemperate as the men. In the end, it was found that the establishment of a public-house became a far lesser evil than its absence.

The amiable enthusiasts I have referred to are doubtless actuated by the best intentions, but their well-meant schemes would only increase the evil they deplore, and accentuate the fact that it is impossible to make people good by Act of Parliament.

FREE TRADE.

THAT England enjoyed a protracted run of prosperity, commencing soon after the introduction of Free Trade, cannot for a moment be denied; and to this fact is probably due the almost superstitious reverence attached to this institution by a large number of people in this country, who apparently regard its doctrines as so many inspirations vouchsafed for the special benefit of the people of England, to be received unhesitatingly and with becoming feelings of veneration and thankfulness. I shall take leave, however, to observe that nothing supernatural has occurred, and that although our guiding star of trade is perfectly visible to all other nations, it is not only generally repudiated by them, but they, one and all, are constantly taking measures to remove themselves farther and farther from its influence. This being so, ought we not at once to abandon the cloak of self-conceit and obstinacy within which we are vainly endeavouring to hide the nakedness of the land, and by relinquishing the meagre comfort derived from this deceptive garment, either place ourselves in a position to regain some of the material prosperity we have lost, or prove to demonstration that the light we are guided by is reliable, and not the mere reflection of a "Will-o'-the-wisp," leading us farther and farther from solid ground, and nearer and nearer to the centre of the bog from which its existence is derived? A thorough examination of the subject would include, among others, the discussion of the following questions, to which, for the present purpose, I shall confine myself.

1st. Did Mr. Cobden advocate the continuance, under existing circumstances, of the system which he inaugurated?

It is perfectly well known that he never for a moment suggested that it could be maintained for any length of time unless adopted by foreign countries. His argument was this: "Let England adopt a policy of Free Trade, exposing the attendant blessings to the full gaze of foreign nations, and the general adoption of its principles must almost immediately follow, and protection will become a thing of the past." This clearly shows that Free Trade originated on a gigantic misconception of its consequential results, and that this country is at present reposing blind confidence in a system which is wanting in the very fundamental principle which was supposed to justify its creation.

2nd. How is the increased prosperity which followed the repeal of the Corn Laws to be explained, except upon the supposition that it was the result of Free Trade?

The answer is, that simultaneously with the change of law, the country obtained an enormous advantage over foreign nations by the introduction of railways at a period in which the various products of the said nations were mostly conveyed by means of horses and carts, and that our increase in prosperity was the direct result of this circumstance.

Now that all this has been changed, and other countries have provided themselves with railways and railway charges, which have entirely reversed the relative positions, and left England with a far dearer means of transit than any other commercial country in the world, we have an opportunity of reviewing our position, and estimating the value of Free Trade when shorn of the adventitious aid which accompanied its inauguration.

3rd. If the principles of Free Trade are sound, why do we continue to tax certain goods coming into this country?

The only possible reason is, that the country is in want of the money derived from the taxes; but this answer completely annihilates the doctrine of Free Trade. If the country is deriving so much nourishment from five-sixths of a loaf, why should it be deprived of the remaining portion? If the advantages derived from the abolition of the old protective duties so far outweighed the value of the revenue receipts, it is difficult to see why the abolition of the remaining portion would not be productive of similar results. If, on the other hand, our present system of obtaining a little money by the taxing of certain goods is a correct one, the reason which prevents our obtaining a little more money by an extension of the process is not particularly obvious.

4th. What steps do we take to convince foreign nations of the truths of the doctrine of Free Trade?

Having placed ourselves on a sufficient pedestal, we proceed to address them somewhat in this way: "We allow you to send goods into this country free, although you tax those we send to you. You doubtless imagine that we are foolish enough thus to allow you to obtain the advantage; but you can make no greater mistake, for the course we are adopting is compelling you indirectly to play into our hands, however much you may labour under a different impression. The fact that our manufacturing industries are steadily passing into your hands in consequence of the system we have adopted, does not in the least interfere with the confidence we repose in it, but merely illustrates the extreme subtlety of the reasoning process by which we arrived at its conclusion."

Having harangued them more or less distinctly in this style, we descend from our pedestal, and, approaching them cap in hand, we continue our address in somewhat altered tones. We say, "Although it is true that by taxing our goods you are injuring yourselves, and very materially assisting us, we trust you will not overdo the thing; we do not require too much assistance of the kind; therefore, pray do not ruin yourselves all at once, and make us rich too suddenly; but rather allow these results to come about slowly and naturally, by admitting our goods on your lowest scale of charges, or, in other words, give us what are popularly and erroneously supposed to be 'most favoured nation clauses.'"

5th. What are the outward and visible signs of the effects of Free Trade in England?

The closing of iron furnaces and iron manufactories, the laying waste of large tracts of agricultural land, the paralysis of general trade caused by the loss of one market after another, and the enormous increase of imports over exports.

6th. How are the outward and visible signs of protection in foreign countries shown?

In the ability of these countries to manufacture their own necessaries if they possess the raw material, and if not, to purchase it in England, and still to retain the power of manufacturing at a lower rate than that at which the finished article could be supplied to them. Also in their ability to buy English iron, manufacture it, send it back to England in the shape of bridges, girders, ship plates, rails, etc., and to undersell the English makers in the home markets, notwithstanding that the iron has been subjected to the cost of carriage both in the outward and homeward journeys!

7th. How are working men affected?

It follows that all the money paid to foreign

workmen for the manufacture of these articles ought to have gone into the pockets of English working men. England possesses the richest mineral fields in the world, with coal and iron lying in close proximity to each other, and adjacent to magnificent seaports; and with these enormous advantages, it is ridiculous to suppose that under equal laws any European country could successfully compete with her for one moment.

8th. The advocates of Free Trade having declared that its introduction would cause this country to become "a paradise for working men," how has this prophecy been fulfilled?

The result is, that the English Government is constantly called upon to assist the working man to leave the kingdom, in order that in America and other protected countries he may find employment, by assisting in producing the food and manufacturing the articles of commerce required by the people who remain in his native land.

9th. These facts being sufficiently notorious, and affecting as they do the very life blood of the country, how does it happen that they receive so little attention from Parliament?

The answer is, that the Government is too much

engaged with the various "burning questions," eternally emanating from philosophic Radicalism, to have sufficient time for the consideration of such prosaic matters as the ordinary industries of the country or its waning trade. They seem to consider that the offer of a ballot box sufficient satisfaction to a people who are crying for bread; and, besides this, there is a kind of unwritten compact between the hundred and seven railway directors and the Government, that neither side shall materially interfere with the other.

The former are what may be termed professional free-traders, who mechanically puff its doctrines both in and out of the House of Commons, and their statements are received by the public as carrying the weight naturally attached to the opinions of so many and independent men of business. But the fact is overlooked that these railway directors are not only supporting the system introduced under a misconception by Mr. Cobden, but the infinitely more serious one inaugurated by themselves, and tacked on to it. In contending that the countries which tax British goods should be allowed to send their own goods into Britain, and that these goods should be subsidized as against the home producer by a bounty in the shape of reduced railway charges, they are extending the doctrines of Free Trade to a point of absurdity unequalled in the annals of commerce, and one which, when thoroughly understood, is not likely to find a single independent supporter in this country.

This, however, being distinctly the railway theory, is it reasonable to suppose that gentlemen who, in the interests of their monopolies, subsidize foreign goods, will consent to these goods being taxed by the State, or that the public can regard the opinions expressed by them in favour of Free Trade as unbiassed and independent testimony? Yet it is on the good sense and integrity of this compact body (supported by a large number of members of Parliament, who are directly or indirectly dependent on railways for contracts or other material advantages) that the country is relying for an impartial judgment on its policy of Free Trade, and which, notwithstanding the overwhelming evidence to the contrary, apparently justifies it in believing that its continuance is an essential element in the future prosperity of this kingdom.

To sum up the whole question, it is abundantly clear that the system we have stumbled on involves a palpable fallacy. If our one-sided system of Free Trade possesses the virtues its advocates claim for it, we ought at once to abolish all import duties of every sort and kind, as well as all commercial treaties. If, on the other hand, we find that the taxation to which English goods are subjected by foreign nations acts disastrously on our trade and commerce, we ought at once to take such steps of reprisal as will either compel them to discontinue the practice, or will enable us, by adopting a similar policy in the matter of protection, to make full use of the superior natural advantages with which this country is so richly endowed, for the purpose of wresting from them the markets of which we have been deprived.

RAILWAY DIRECTORS IN PARLIAMENT.

THE chairman of the London and North-Western Railway Company, in addressing the shareholders of that company for the half-year ending December, 1880, made use of these remarkable words :—

<small>CHAIRMAN OF LONDON AND NORTH-WESTERN RAILWAY COMPANY.</small>
"As they were aware, Government and Parliament to railway people meant ill-treatment and oppression. They did not look for any good from them. On the contrary, every year they had rather increased the burdens of Railway Companies. The railway interest had hitherto borne the treatment, and been content with the British grumble, but sooner or later they would all have to combine, and when they did, no matter what Government was in power, the interests of the share and debenture holders, and people who were depending for their living on railway working, were so powerful that no Government could afford to say they would not attend to them."

The threat contained in these words is no idle one, and the railway monopolists who direct the power obtained from the possession of more than seven hundred million of capital, have already laid the foundation for carrying it into effect. They have engaged as their salaried servants fifty-one members of the House of Lords and one hundred and seven members of the House of Commons, and there is nothing in the present state of the law to prevent them from retaining in a similar capacity every member of both Houses. No wonder the gentleman who presides over one hundred millions of the aforesaid capital feels himself strong enough to threaten, and his threat may probably explain the apparent apathy of this otherwise terribly reforming Government of ours. It may have induced Mr. Chamberlain to come to the conclusion that "railways must know their own business best," and have caused him to hint to his zealous official that a few soothing words (calculated to allay any feeling of anxiety on the part of the public) would not be out of place.

But granting the expediency of this line of conduct from a safety point of view, what becomes of the consistency? How is it that institutions are constantly singled out for Radical attack simply because they are termed "anomalies," and with absolutely nothing else against them?

Mr. Chamberlain would disestablish the Church because it is an anomaly! I ask if there can be conceived a greater anomaly than that railway directors are allowed an absolutely unlimited right to sit in Parliament, and from that place to decree the amount of protection which shall be accorded to the public against Railway Companies; and I ask if it is possible to imagine an anomaly fraught with greater danger to the public weal? It means that the sieve through which the entire trade and agriculture of this kingdom has to pass, either directly or indirectly, is held by railway directors, and that *from their place in Parliament they determine the size of the mesh.* As an illustration of the solidity of the railway power and the use made of it in Parliament, I cannot do better than quote from the speech of the chairman of the Hull and Barnsley Railway Company, in addressing his shareholders at the last half-yearly meeting of the company, in reference to a Bill which that company had occasion to promote with respect to the payment of certain interest. He says :—

"Of course the Interest Bill was delayed a year, in consequence of this vexed question of standing orders, but the moment the standing orders were altered in the House of Commons, there was no objection to the Interest Bill coming forward. It did come forward, and we were met with opposition where we least expected. I did think, after the fight had been lost and won, that there was a reasonable prospect that we might have lived in amity with the North-Eastern, but the North-Eastern turned up in the House of Commons in the shape of Sir J. Pease, Bart.,* and after making a very acrimonious speech, in which he charged us with everything short of actual dishonesty—indeed, I am not quite sure whether he did not charge us with that—sheltered under the privilege of Parliament, he succeeded in throwing out a Bill which was a mere act of justice to Messrs. Lucas and Aird. Of course, I have to be careful in the remarks I make, because I know what the privilege of Parliament is; but it seems to me that people are entitled to do, under the privileges of Parliament, things which in private life would be looked upon as very questionable taste, and would call forth much stronger remarks than those I shall be justified in making. I do not think it will be to

_{CHAIRMAN OF HULL AND BARNSLEY RAILWAY COMPANY.}

* This is the same gentleman previously alluded to as Mr. Pease, he having been recently made a Baronet.

CHAIRMAN OF HULL AND BARNSLEY RAILWAY COMPANY. our interests, and it is certainly not my duty, to travel over the many allegations, most of which—nine-tenths of which—were hopelessly incorrect, that Sir J. Pease made against us. The only one remark that I ought to make is, that Sir J. Pease, on a previous occasion, distinctly promised to support our Bill; and when it came to the time he turned round and took an opposite course. I do not think Sir J. Pease was justified in doing that. I do not think the House of Commons thought he was justified in doing that, nor do I think he was justified in saying all the many things he did against our company, which really did not arise on the merits of the Bill, but which were a sort of rambling indictment against the company, which I think we may very well afford to disregard. The motion was seconded by Mr. Cropper, a director of the Midland Railway Company; and I may tell you that the manager of the Great Northern told me he had from these railway directors in the House of Commons, who were interested in such matters, *no fewer than one hundred and thirty-six promises to vote against us.* Of course that shows what the power of the railway directors is in the House. Well, I am a railway director myself, and I am in the House of Commons myself. If it is on any future occasion proposed that the votes of railway directors, or even shareholders, should not be allowed in the House of Commons on matters in which they have a distinct interest, I for one, railway director as I am, shall vote in favour of the proposition."

<small>CHAIRMAN OF HULL AND BARNSLEY RAILWAY COMPANY.</small>

It will be remembered that the Hull and Barnsley is the railway previously alluded to as almost the sole instance of an independent competing main line passed by Parliament for nearly a quarter of a century, and it is therefore apparently regarded by the other companies as an interloper, against which they consider it right to make common cause.

Referring again to the remarks of the chairman of the London and North-Western Railway Company, no one will dispute for a moment the power and wealth of Railway Companies, and indeed the fact is only too notorious. At the same time, it must not be overlooked that the traders and agriculturists possess more wealth and far greater power, if they only know how to use it. The real power of the Railway Companies has been derived from the ignorance of the public with respect to their rights, and to the general confusion which has resulted. Once let the people understand the law and the way in which it is systematically overridden and defied, then, no matter how many millions the Railway Companies possess, or how enormous their influence in Parliament, the people of this country will not allow matters to remain as they are. By "people," I mean not only the traders and agriculturists, but the working men. No class is more deeply affected by this question than they. The present system is not only playing into the hands of foreign capitalists, but of foreign working men, and work which ought to be done by Englishmen is now performed by foreigners. If the employer cannot make ends meet, how is it possible he can advance the wages of his workpeople, or even continue to pay them at the present rate? On every side we hear of depression in trade and reductions in wages, and this state of things has existed not merely for short periods, but for years and years, with apparently no prospect of change. At the same time, we see the traffic receipts of the Railway Companies steadily increasing, whilst that traffic is charged generally at the highest rates ever known. The facts being sufficiently notorious, Railway Companies must remember that, even if they have succeeded in overawing the Government, there is a considerable power in the country with which they will have to deal, and in a fight for supremacy they are hardly likely to get the best of it.

SUGGESTED REMEDIES.

1st. That the House of Commons should refuse to consider any Bill promoted by a Railway Company having any one or more of its directors members of the House of Lords; and that such company should have no *locus standi* before committees of the House of Commons, for any purpose whatsoever.

2nd. That no Railway Company be allowed to have more than one director in the House of Commons, and then only in cases where the entire capital of the company amounts to five millions or over.

3rd. That no member of Parliament be allowed to accept the office of director to any Railway

Company without being compelled to appeal to his constituency.

4th. That at the next general election, the constituencies do not return railway directors, except upon otherwise very strong grounds.

With regard to the first two of these suggestions, my reason for drawing a distinction between the House of Lords and the House of Commons is this, viz. that it may be urged on behalf of the Railway Companies—and, I think, fairly—that, as traders and others sit in the House of Commons, and have the power of introducing Bills affecting Railway Companies, it is only fair that the latter should have an opportunity of stating their views on the questions involved. But traders, etc., do not, as a rule, sit in the House of Lords. Most of the peers are railway shareholders (and, indeed, in this way railway interests are fairly protected in the Commons), so that it may be taken for granted that nothing will be done in the Upper House which would press unfairly on railway interests. On the other hand, to allow Railway Companies to be represented in the Lords, where the trader is excluded, is manifestly improper to the last degree.

With regard to the third suggestion, the plan now adopted by the companies is to wait until an individual has been elected a member of Parliament, and then to offer him a seat on their Board. There can hardly be a doubt that the constituency should be allowed the opportunity of saying whether or not they approve of the acceptance of the appointment.

As to the last suggestion, nothing, in my opinion, will call the attention of the Government to the necessity of railway reform more pointedly than to find the present number of directors very materially diminished at the next election. It is hardly probable that any Government can with safety disregard the solid vote of one hundred and seven members of Parliament.

RAILWAY COMMISSIONERS' COURT.

THE chairman of the London and North-Western Company, in pursuance of the remarks to which I have alluded, proceeded to say:—

<small>CHAIRMAN OF THE LONDON AND NORTH-WESTERN COMPANY.</small> "First, they have the Railway Commissioners, a standing monument to the repudiation of national engagements by the Parliament of this country, with powers for exacting rates, which the highest authority stated was equivalent to confiscation, and they were a standing menace to this great property."

It would have been extremely instructive had the respected chairman entered a little more fully into particulars, and given his hearers some idea of the "national engagements" to which he referred, and whose repudiation had become typified by the fact that powers originally vested in the Court of Common Pleas had been transferred to the Railway Commissioners. It would have been well also if the name of the highest authority had been given, as the public would be naturally interested in knowing who the gentleman was who had expressed the opinion that the mere fact of giving Railway Commissioners powers to exact rates in accordance with Acts of Parliament (the Acts being in existence long previous to their appointment) was equivalent to confiscation. There is only one statement in the above-mentioned remarks to which I can agree, and that is the one describing the Railway Commissioners' Court as a "standing menace to the great property." This it certainly is where the companies act in defiance of law, but, unfortunately, in the great majority of instances, there the matter ends; there is a "menace" and nothing more!

Surely, the following list of rates (originally compiled by the *Mark Lane Express*), published in the *Times* on the very day on which the London and North-Western chairman's speech appeared, is sufficient proof of the truth of my assertion, and forcibly illustrates the way in which Railway Companies have "kept faith" with Parliament:—

LIST OF RATES.
GUANO AND PACKED MANURE.

From Petersfield to	Charge for Guano and Packed Manure. Per ton. s. d.	Maximum rate. s. d.	Amount of overcharge per cent.
Nine Elms	12 6	9 0	39
Wimbledon	13 4	8 2	63
Woking	10 0	5 4	87
Guildford	9 2	4 4	111
Whitley	6 8	3 0	122
Haslemere	5 10	2 0	191
Liphook	5 0	1 6	233
Liss	4 2	1 0	316
Rogate	5 0	1 0	400
Elstead	5 0	1 2	342
Midhurst	5 10	1 8	250
Rowland's Castle	5 0	1 6	233
Havant	5 10	1 10½	218
Aldershot	11 8	6 10	70
Farnham	9 2	6 0	52
Alton	10 10	7 7½	42
Ropley	12 6	8 8¼	44
Alresford	13 4	7 9	72
Basingstoke	13 4	9 0	48
Winchester	10 0	6 4½	58
Bishopstoke	9 2	5 2¼	77
Fareham	6 8	3 4	100
Porchester	6 8	2 10½	134
Cosham	6 8	2 6¼	160
Portsmouth	7 6	3 0	150
Chandler's Ford	9 2	5 6½	60
Downton	15 10	10 3	54
Poole	15 0	13 2	13
Salisbury	16 8	8 11	86
Windsor	13 4	8 7	55
Reading	15 0	10 5	44
Gosport	7 6	4 2	80
Andover	15 0	9 5	59
Milford	7 6	3 3	130
Southampton	10 0	6 2	74
Bishop's Waltham	10 0	6 0	66
Mottisfont	18 4	8 2	124
Exeter	40 0	24 0	66

Now, persons who pay rates three or four times in excess of the legal ones can hardly be supposed to do so from choice, and when it is remembered that Mr. Hickman, the largest ironmaster in South Staffordshire, deliberately told the Select Committee that he was afraid to invoke the protection of the Railway Commissioners' Court, farmers and small traders can hardly be expected to make much use of it.

Acts of Parliament which relate to undue preference and " reasonable " terminals, etc., etc., are, with reference to these people, simply a farce, if the only means of enforcing compliance is by the aid of the Railway Commissioners. If these acts are for the future to be anything more than the dead letter they have been in the past, it is the duty of Parliament to see that it is within the power of the humblest trader or farmer to obtain the protection which they were passed for the purpose of affording.

I now propose to give my readers a practical illustration of the position of the farmer under the present railway system, and then to point out what that position would be if the equal mileage and equal terminal system were in force, and I may add that all I say with respect to the former applies with equal force to almost every trader in the land.

Now, suppose a farmer finds out that the terminal charges on his different kinds of produce, instead of being reasonable, as provided in the Acts, are unreasonable, and that he is rich enough and heroic enough to fight the question before the Railway Commissioners. Let us, for argument's sake, say he commences with raising the question of the terminal charges on "hops" at a certain station, and that he brings his suit to a successful issue. All he has done is to decide the amount of terminals at one particular station on one particular article of produce. As, however, the terminal costs vary (according to the Railway Companies) at different places, he would have to prosecute almost as many suits as there are stations on the company's system, in order to decide the proper terminals on hops. The company would be in possession of all information with respect to terminal costs, varying at the different places, and they would be able to produce it at the critical moment without his having either the time or opportunity of bringing rebutting evidence.

Let us suppose, however, an ideal farmer, rich

enough and lucky enough to come triumphantly through this exhaustive ordeal, what would be his position? He would then have to go through the whole process again with regard to potatoes, and so on with regard to every article of produce in which he dealt. I say that Acts of Parliament which cannot be enforced, except under such circumstances, are simply an incumbrance to the statute book.

Let us see the position of the same individual, if the equal mileage and equal terminal system were in force. He would refer to the Railway Company's published list of rates, and look out "hops." He would at once see that the charge was so much per ton per mile for any distance—or that the charge was so much per ton per mile for five miles, so much per ton per mile for ten miles—so much per ton per mile for any further distance, exactly as the company had thought fit (within their powers) to fix it. He would then look out the terminal charges per ton upon hops, and, by adding this to the number of miles, he would have the exact rate to any place he wished to reach.

If, in addition to this, he required the hops to be carted a certain distance, he would have to add on the charge per ton per mile for cartage, as quoted in the published list with reference to hops. In case the company charged him more than his calculations amounted to, he would simply have to go before the nearest bench of magistrates or County Court judge, and by producing the company's list prove his case.

Suppose, however, that the company's list claimed terminals where they had no right to them, or mileage rates in excess of their maximum mileage rates, the farmer would not individually be called upon to dispute the matter with the Railway Company. The mere publication of illegal claims of this description would at once call the attention of all persons, interested in the particular traffic affected, to the subject. They would all suffer equally in proportion to their trade, and would probably lose very little time in making common cause for the purpose of trying a test case before the Railway Commissioners, which would settle the question, over the entire system of the company proceeded against. The farmer would then have the satisfaction of knowing that even if untaxed foreign produce is allowed to compete with home produce, the former would no longer receive a heavy bounty on its arrival in this country; also that he and his brother farmers would be relieved from the payment of the said bounty, and that for the first time Englishmen and foreigners would possess equal right over English railways.

Under the proposed system, it is clear that any body of traders or farmers would be enabled to try a question of mileage or terminal charges before the Railway Commissioners, but there would still remain the question of cartage, on which the latter would only have jurisdiction in case of inequality. The Railway Companies might fix the cartage at any rate per mile they chose, as there are no Acts of Parliament regulating the rate. This, however, would be a matter of no importance, because the public would, if the rates were fixed too high, probably do their own cartage, and in this way compete on equal terms with the companies, always provided that the Railway Commissioners have full power to order that the public have every reasonable convenience afforded to them for the purpose of this work.

Now, even if the system I have suggested were in force, it would still be within the power of the

Railway Companies to render the Equality Acts as useless as they are at present, viz. by making secret allowances or drawbacks to the foreigner or favoured trader. The drawback system has been adopted to an enormous extent in the past, and it is for this reason that I have proposed in the "Suggested Remedies," in the chapter on "Undue Preference," that the Railway Commissioners shall be vested with the most ample powers for dealing with it, and that the penalties shall be severe enough to make it quite out of the question that any Railway Company could adopt it. At present, the Railway Commissioners' Court has no power to award damages. A trader who proves he has been subjected to loss, in consequence of illegal rates, can only obtain from that court an injunction to restrain for the future the illegality complained of. He has then to commence proceedings in the ordinary courts for his damages, and in this way the whole proceedings probably last as many years as they ought to last weeks. It is abundantly obvious that a railway court should have power to award damages, and thus determine the whole question involved at one and the same time.

At present there is no appeal from the Railway

Commissioners' Court. This, in my opinion, is neither fair to the public, the Railway Companies, nor to the court itself. The court consists of three members, viz. one lawyer and two laymen, and, considering the momentous nature of the questions it is called upon to decide, this tribunal, from a legal point of view, can hardly be regarded as a strong one. Its decision seems, therefore, to be looked upon as fair subjects of attack by railway directors, either in or out of Parliament.

Then, again, railway counsel are very fond of animadverting on them, and sometimes in rather insulting terms; and as they possess the advantage of being able to describe the case in a very different way to that in which it was presented to the commissioners, it is no difficult matter to produce a very erroneous impression.

Now, all this sort of thing would be impossible if the decisions could be appealed against. The public, too, have noticed in the commissioners' judgments a tendency towards compromise, and, for this reason, some of the judgments appear somewhat lacking in consistency. This tends to create a feeling of uncertainty, not so much as to the law as to the particular view the commissioners may or may not take on the matters in issue, and prevents people from risking a trial, from the result of which there is no appeal, and which, if wrong, will give legal sanction in perpetuity to an illegality. Considering the ruthless way in which the commissioners' decisions (adverse to Railway Companies) are systematically attacked, it can hardly be wondered at that in certain cases the Court tries its best to please both parties, the result being that it ends in pleasing neither. It is therefore highly desirable that the Commissioners' decisions, either on questions of law or fact, should be subject to one appeal, and that the appeal should be to the House of Lords. Questions would then be definitely settled and the law rendered perfectly clear, and both the public and the Railway Companies would have a much better idea of their respective rights than they now possess.

TRADERS' "LOCUS STANDI" BEFORE PARLIAMENTARY COMMITTEES.

ALTHOUGH I have previously commented on the remarkable absence of any demand for railway reform on the part of those who may be termed professional agitators, I must not omit to mention that there were several Liberals on the Select Committee on Railway Rates and Fares, who contrasted considerably with some other members of the same party on the Committee in the great services they rendered on behalf of the public. One of these gentlemen was Mr. B. Samuelson, on whose motion the committee was granted, and who, as previously mentioned, would have been appointed chairman, had not the railway directors, by one vote, succeeded in placing Mr. Ashley in that position. Mr. Samuelson now proposes that when Railway Companies apply to Parliament for increased powers of any description, it shall be open to all traders or persons affected by their existing rates to appear before the committee and object, on the ground that the companies are making unwarrantable and oppressive use of their existing powers, and to ask the committee to refuse to add to them until they are carried out in accordance with the spirit of the law as well as the letter.

This proposition is perfectly consistent with the opinion I have previously expressed, that the rights the companies possess cannot now be interfered with, and must remain with them. But, on the other hand, if Parliament ascertains that the companies are using these powers for purposes altogether improper, or foreign to those for which they were given, it has a perfect right to say, "You may keep what you have, but no further assistance will be rendered until the powers with which you have been entrusted are used in a reasonable manner, and in the spirit in which Parliament intended."

The instances referred to in the chapter on "Short Distance Clauses" (where Railway Companies are shown to use a few hundred yards of railway line as a lever for extorting black-mail) afford an excellent illustration of the kind of business which would be brought under the notice of the committee.

Then, again, there are cases in which Railway Companies are guilty of breaches of faith to Parliament itself.

Mr. Hickman describes how the Midland Railway Company obtained powers to make a line into Staffordshire by sending their manager, Mr. Allport, to tell the committee that the rates of the existing companies were too high, and that if the Midland Company were allowed to make their line, these rates would be reduced; and how, when the railway was made, the Midland Company joined "the ring," and charged the same rates as the other companies. Surely, the traders should, in cases of this kind, have a right to appear before committees, and ask them not to add to the powers of companies who so greatly misuse those they already possess!

It will, doubtless, be urged that committees will not have the time to enter into matters of this description. If that be so, the remedy must be by special or "Traders' Committees," who shall be appointed for the express purpose of hearing objections to any railway Bills before Parliament.

This will not interfere with the companies in their proceedings before the ordinary committee, but will simply mean that before any railway Bill can become law, it will be necessary that the Traders' Committee be satisfied. The work, however, of the committee would not be great, because in nineteen times out of twenty the Railway Companies would compromise with the trader or farmer rather than go before it. The tribunal would simply amount to a Court of Equity or Revision, without power "to take from," but with power to refuse "to add to." The trading and agricultural classes are under a deep debt of gratitude to Mr. Samuelson for his public-spirited policy, not only in regard to the Select Committee, but for this particularly practical suggestion, for enabling existing grievances and breaches of faith to be brought directly under the notice of Parliament.

COMPETING RAILWAY BILLS IN PARLIAMENT.

THE fact that no new competing trunk line has been sanctioned by Parliament for nearly a quarter of a century (with the exception of the Hull and Barnsley Railway), is the direct consequence of the decision of a Parliamentary Committee some twenty years ago.

This decision, which practically annihilated competition and divided the whole country among the existing Railway Companies, was given in reference to a Bill introduced by the Great Eastern Company, for powers to connect their system with the Yorkshire coal-fields, for the purpose of bringing Yorkshire coal to the metropolis. It was shown that, owing to the remarkably level character of the intervening country and the consequently easy gradients, the Great Eastern Railway Company would be able to carry coal at exceedingly low rates; and the proof of these facts occasioned the loss of the Bill.

The chairman of the committee distinctly stated

it would not be fair to allow a company to possess such exceptional advantages for the transit of coals, and to use them for the purpose of competing directly with the Great Northern Company between Yorkshire and London. The strength of the case having thus justified the rejection of the Bill, and previous decisions having invariably proved fatal to weak cases, promoters were entirely fogged as to the requirements of Parliamentary Committees, and, as a natural sequence, they ceased to promote.

From that time, railway directors have assumed the airs of territorial rulers. They speak of the different districts through which their respective railways pass as of so many principalities, and characterize any attempt on the part of traders to create at their own cost a means of transit for their goods as "attacks" and "unwarrantable invasions" upon their principal prerogatives. These prerogatives, if not upheld by a standing army, are sufficiently protected by an army of "standing counsel," and traders, by their complete inability to provide an equal attacking force, are compelled to see their rights—rights co-existent with the history of trade—usurped by this mushroom power, the growth of less than a quarter of a century!

The Hull and Barnsley Railway Act was the first instance during the period alluded to in which traders succeeded in breaking their chains, and this, as before mentioned, was only passed under exceptional circumstances and after various fruitless attempts dating over a long period of years.

In order to obtain the necessary capital, the promoters advertised that, during the process of construction, interest at the rate of five per cent. would be allowed on all money paid. The British public, well knowing the great value of the undertaking—the line passing as it does through a district described by Mr. John Staat Forbes, of the London, Chatham, and Dover Railway (to the Parliamentary Committee), as the "rich plum of the North-Eastern cake"—subscribed within a few hours nearly three times the required capital!

The Railway Companies, who had exhausted every device to throw the Bill out in committee, next proceeded to obtain the filing of a Bill in Chancery to prevent the payment of interest on the ground of illegality, and the Hull and Barnsley Company had no alternative but to bring forward a Bill in Parliament for the purpose of legalizing this payment. What happened, and how the Bill was defeated, will be gleaned from the remarks of the chairman of the company, quoted in a preceding chapter.

The following illustration will explain the difficulties with which promoters of new Bills are surrounded. We will assume that an Act has been obtained for the construction of a line which is of the most vital importance to the traders, shipowners, agriculturists, and working classes of the vicinity. The capitalist is prepared to find the necessary capital conditionally on his receiving interest during the period of construction, and this interest the promoters are perfectly prepared to pay. At this stage of the proceedings the parties are confronted by an existing and ridiculous law, which ordains that this interest must not be paid. That is to say, that if A provides B with £100 for the purpose of carrying out important works, the law will not allow A to receive £5 back at the end of the year, although B only requires £95, and A wants his £5. Now, by a Parliamentary fiction, this law is supposed to exist for the protection of the public, the contention being that certain persons might otherwise be persuaded to invest their money under the impression that the interest was being earned before the line was made, and in this way be tempted to embark in an unprofitable undertaking. If this species of investor really exists, it seems probable that his money will be safer invested in railway shares than if left to his own unaided intelligence to protect from the allurements of those individuals who, by means of the "confidence trick" and other similar devices, are in the habit of providing investments for capitalists of similar intellectual capacities. However this may be, it follows that the enormous interests involved are set on one side for the ostensible purpose of extending protection to half-witted (and probably mythical) investors; but the law really exists for the protection of existing monopolies, and is maintained by the solid votes of railway directors in Parliament.

These gentlemen thoroughly understand that the public will not invest money in enterprises which take years to complete, and during which period they can receive no interest. Even, therefore, if competing Railway Companies manage to get their Bills through Parliament, it follows almost of necessity that the greatest difficulty is experienced in raising the requisite capital, and, in consequence, the schemes either probably become absorbed by existing monopolies or are allowed to drop.

The law against payment of interest during construction does not, however, touch existing Railway Companies. These people may make a new line, and borrow the necessary capital on the security of their property at any rate of interest at which they can persuade the public to lend it. It is only when similar power is applied for by a new and competing company, that the railway directors assemble in full force and make use of the trusts reposed in them by their constituents, for the purpose of protecting their private interests to the injury of the community at large; or, in other words, they say, "if we cannot crush competing schemes in committee, we can, by our own votes in the House of Commons, prevent the necessary capital from being raised, and so effect our object in another way." No better illustration can be given of the practical working and effects of this action on the part of railway directors than is contained in the descriptive remarks of the chairman of the Hull and Barnsley Railway Company, which are already in the possession of my readers.

The Act authorizing the construction of this railway having been referred to by Sir Thomas Farrer as a proof of the "potential competition of new railways," the fate which befel its direct corollary—the East and West Yorkshire Railway Bill—may be regarded as an equally forcible illustration of the fact that "one swallow does not make a summer."

The passing of the former Act rendered it incumbent on the inhabitants of the extensive coal and industrial district of West Yorkshire to promote a line of their own, in order to join the Hull and Barnsley Railway, and thus escape from the yoke of the North-Eastern Company. The Bill, although opposed by the North-Eastern, Midland, Great Northern, Lancashire and Yorkshire Railway Companies, and one landowner, ultimately passed the Commons, although in a somewhat mutilated form. In the Lords the opposition was withdrawn, with the exception of the North-Eastern Company. Evidence was produced showing that a single colliery company in the district had lost over £200,000 in four years' working. A colliery-owner informed the committee that £80,000 invested in his undertaking would, he feared, be entirely lost unless the line were passed. Mr. Charlesworth, another most extensive coalowner, stated that the railway was of so much importance that his firm were prepared to find £50,000 of the capital, and by the production of a diagram (showing an advance in rates since 1865 of between thirty and fifty per cent.), he adduced most weighty arguments in support of the Bill. I may state that this line was only about twenty-four miles in length, with every landowner in favour of it (excepting the one mentioned), and yet the Bill was thrown out. Thus these coalowners, ironmasters, landowners, farmers, and general traders were forbidden to make a railway over their own land for the conveyance of their own traffic, and were told as in so many words that, in spite of the enormous increase in their rates and the widespread disaster consequent upon it, the huge opposing monopoly must be protected, and that the money spent by the promoters during sixteen days in committee (at a time it could be so ill spared) was all thrown away.

Now, let us turn to the other side of the question. The North-Eastern Company at their next general meeting were congratulated by the chairman on the victory achieved. A dividend of $7\frac{1}{2}$ per cent. was declared, accompanied by an intimation that more could have been paid, as much had been charged to revenue which might have been put to capital, but it was not considered well to pay a higher dividend, because it *encouraged opposition*. This company paid a dividend of $7\frac{1}{2}$ per cent. previous to the great rise in rates in 1870. They have subsequently paid as much as ten, while, for the half-year ending December, 1883, the dividend is at the rate of $8\frac{3}{4}$ per cent.

I may here state that the East and West Yorkshire Bill, being in exceptionally strong hands, was again introduced in the session of 1882, and, after a whole year had been wasted and another enormous sum expended in Parliamentary expenses, it ultimately became law. Now, these Parliamentary expenses simply amount to a scandal, and are caused to a great extent by the deliberate and intentional action of the Railway Companies, in order to crush and frighten away competitors by the sheer weight of money. The companies fully understand that "play" to them means "death" to their opponents. They therefore bring up a host of witnesses, for the purpose of prolonging the cases almost interminably; and by giving counsel prodigious retaining fees, with daily refreshers, they not only cause the expenses to assume frightful proportions, but, in compelling their opponents to incur similar costs, rely on the pace being made too warm for them, or that the scheme, even if passed, may be thus seriously crippled for want of funds. As an instance in point, the promoters of the Manchester Ship Canal were last year obliged to obtain £100,000 for Parliamentary expenses. Their Bill was thrown out, and this year a similar item will have to be added to the cost of an undertaking which is absolutely necessary, unless our Lancashire manufacturing trade is to be handed over bodily to the foreigner. Thus, to the end of the chapter, this work will be burdened with the interest on these sums, which, as a matter of course, will come out of the pockets of the traders using the canal.

In the case of smaller companies, these expenses often amount to fifteen or twenty per cent. of their entire capital. Before ground was broken for the purpose of making their railway, the Great Northern Company were compelled to expend in Parliamentary expenses no less a sum than £420,000, and the interest, simple and compound, on this sum now amounts to nearly £2,500,000 of entirely wasted money, upon which interest is secured from the public by the exaction of rates which are destroying the trade of the country. Now, taking all these circumstances into consideration, and putting the question of free trade, to which I shall shortly have to refer, on one side, it is well to look matters in the face, and inquire what it is that British traders and agriculturists are now attempting to do. They are trying to compete with foreign countries, and having for a long time been closely pressed, are now rapidly losing market after market. One of their chief competitors is America, and in that country, although there is protection in home against foreign productions, there is complete free trade in railway carriage, the consent of Congress for the making of new railways not being necessary. All that a Railway Company has to do after formation is to schedule so much land, and give notice to the owners that it is intended to purchase it for railway purposes, either by private contract, or valuation, or on the ordinary principle of arbitration.

Such company may lay down rails side by side with the line of an existing company, so long as one hundred feet clear is left between them, and in this way compete with it as absolutely and directly as two opposing shopkeepers compete in this country. The result of this system is that grain is now carried from Chicago to New York, a distance of 950 miles, at 35 cents gold per 100 lbs., or 17½ per cental English money, equal to 28s. per ton. This being the result of free trade in carriage, I will now give a few instances of the result of protection, as exemplified in this country, as follows :—

Produce.	Places.	Distance carried.	Rates.
		Miles.	Per ton. £ s. d.
Potatoes..................	Northwich to Manchester	18	0 6 8
Artificial manure in two ton loads	Stockton to Darlington	11½	0 5 0
Ditto, in quantities of less than two tons......	Ditto	11½	0 6 3
Fish, by passenger train at company's risk	Montrose to Glasgow	117	4 0 0
Wool	Bradford to Banbury	142	2 0 0
Grain	Redhill to Croydon	12	0 3 4
Ditto	Croydon to Merstham	10	0 3 9
Butter...	Fermoy to Cork	38	0 15 6
Coal	Munster to Tipperary	24	0 5 0
Goods of the highest class	Dublin to Mullingar	50¼	1 18 4
Ditto	Clonsilla to Dublin	7	0 9 2
Ditto	Roscommon to Dublin	96	3 10 10
Goods of the sixth class	Castlebar to Dublin	150	5 8 4
Ditto, fifth class	Newbridge to Dublin	25	0 13 4

If we compare the grain rate from Merstham to Croydon with the grain rate from Chicago to New York, it seems that *the English farmer is paying for carriage £17 16s., where the American farmer pays 28s.* In addition to this, on all articles of agriculture necessary to the production of grain, the difference in the rate of carriage may be reasonably supposed to be at least as great, and probably (as in the case of manure) is in some instances considerably larger. To these differences we have to add the heavy bounty in the shape of reduced rates given to the American grain on its arrival in England. Now, if my readers will kindly bear in mind that what applies to grain applies to nearly every other article of agricultural produce, and to all materials incidental to farming operations, and that the circumstances affecting farming apply in a greater or less degree to every trade in the kingdom, they will be able to form a more or less accurate notion of the hopeless character of the struggle in which our commerce and agriculture are engaged.

It may be, doubtless, urged that in taking grain as an example, I have fixed upon an extreme case, and compared a short distance with a long one; but

I ask, Can any possible mitigation of the facts on this score materially affect the question? Even supposing the differences only amounted to a half, or even a quarter of those shown, is it reasonable to suppose that our country can cope with them? In America, pig-iron is carried from Chattanoago to St. Louis, 1000 miles, for 19s. per ton; and in Great Britain, it is carried from Blaenavon to Govilon, $10\frac{1}{4}$ miles, for 5s. per ton; and still people wonder why trade is leaving the country!

SUGGESTED REMEDIES.

1st. That Railway Companies shall have power to pay interest on capital during the course of the construction of their lines.

2nd. That promoters shall be entitled to construct a railway on proving before a committee that three-fourths of the landowners are favourable —even although the projected railway shall run within a few hundred yards, and parallel to an existing railway. The committee to have power to divert the course of the said proposed railway in such manner as in the interests of the opposing landowners they may think fit.

3rd. That no Railway Company shall have a *locus standi* before any committee for the purpose of opposing a new railway, unless the promoters propose running powers over, or junction with, the aforesaid company's railway, and that in such case the aforesaid Railway Company shall be strictly limited to evidence showing the practical inconvenience or danger of the aforesaid running powers or junctions.

Having already sufficiently explained the nature and effects of the law prohibiting the payment of interest, I do not consider it necessary to make any further observations on this head; but with regard to my second proposition, in order to give a practical illustration to my meaning, I will take the case of the Staffordshire iron trade. My readers will remember that it was stated in evidence before the Select Committee that the trade was threatened with extinction, and that the number of furnaces had decreased from 110 in 1862 to 41 in 1882.

Mr. Hickman, in his evidence, says, "I would just illustrate the way in which Railway Companies treat us, by giving you a few instances. From

Deepfields to Birmingham, Monument Lane Station, the distance is nine miles two chains, and the rate is 2*s*. 6*d*. per ton for pig-iron; the maximum legal charge would be 1*s*. 3¾*d*.; so that we pay 1*s*. 2¼*d*. above the legal rate. Then, to Dudley, which is all London and North-Western, a distance of four miles two chains, the rate is 2*s*. 6*d*., whereas it should be sevenpence, the excess being 1*s*. 11*d*."

Now, if Mr. Hickman and his brother ironmasters, with a certain proportion of landowners, had the power to go to the Railway Company and say, "If you don't at once reduce your rates from Deepfields to Birmingham and to Dudley, we will make a railway, and not only carry our own traffic, but compete with you for yours," and if other people all over the country could act in the same way, this iniquitous system which is now paralyzing our industries would probably come to an end. Of course, I am presuming that the "equal mileage for equal distance" system is enforced; otherwise, in the case I have quoted, the London and North-Western Company would simply reduce their own rates to a minimum to places affected by the new line, and so crush it in the same way as they now crush the sea competition. On the other hand, if a reduction in the mileage rates to these places entailed a similar reduction all over their system, "the game" would not be "worth the candle," or if it were, the public would reap a very material advantage by the general reduction.

The third proposition directly involves the question of domestic protection, and may be summed up thus, viz. "Is that portion of our carrying trade performed by the use of engines, trucks, and iron rails, to be artificially protected against the remaining portion, and also against every other trade in the kingdom?" The railway directors will reply, "Yes; and if you prevent us from appearing before committees and stating whether or no new railways are in our opinion justified by the amount of trade in particular districts, it will end in unproductive railways being made."

The obvious answer is, What does it matter to the public, so long as they obtain cheap rates? If the people who make our iron, raise our coal, manufacture our necessaries, and produce our food, are compelled to compete with one another and rely on their own individual efforts to make their undertakings pay, on what conceivable principle can the people whose business it is to carry their productions be asked to be relieved from the operation of the universal law?

Let us suppose that the consent of Parliament were a condition precedent to the establishment of new iron works, and that Parliament consisted chiefly of ironmasters and their immediate friends. Let us suppose that the owners of existing iron works were entitled to appear before committees of such Parliament, for the purpose of expressing their opinions as to the necessity for the proposed new works; does it not follow that the price of iron would be as far in excess of its present value as the cost of railway carriage is now in excess of its real value?

The artificial nature of our present railway system is nowhere more clearly shown than in the dividends and stocks of the different companies. In America, the dividends and stocks of Railway Companies rise and fall with those of other trades, in a perfectly natural manner; but in England, they continue to rise when the trades from which the dividends come are being carried on either at no profit or at an absolute loss.

When the general trade-glass of this country

points to "very stormy," the railway glass stands almost continually at "set fair." But the end must come! The process of "killing the goose which lays the golden eggs" cannot last for ever; and the question now before the country is, Shall Parliament step in at once and arrest the operation, or allow it to continue to the ultimate ruin of all concerned?

PROPOSED SHIPPING LEGISLATION.

THE shipping trade has been almost the only one for many years past to show any symptoms of vitality, and possibly this may be accounted for by the fact that, of all our industries, it has been least affected by English laws.

Shipowners, however, have recently complained much of the oppressive action of the Board of Trade, and it now seems probable that the prevailing Radical blight is about to descend upon them, and one more nail is to be driven into the coffin of British commerce.

Mr. Chamberlain has already made public the outlines of a measure affecting shipowners, having previously prepared the mind of the nation for a calm and judicial inquiry, by bringing a charge of wholesale murder against them, and no sooner does the President of the Board of Trade insert the knife, than the Permanent Secretary rushes forward to turn it round.

Now, however much one may disagree with Sir Thomas Farrer, it must be granted that this operation has certainly the merit of consistency for having previously been at great pains to inform the public that Railway Companies should be allowed to crush the shipowner wherever they find him, it seems only natural that he should proffer the assistance of the Board of Trade for the object in view.

Accordingly, a departmental notice, signed "Board of Trade," has been published of a most sensational character, reminding one more of a transpontine "tragedy" than a sober official document, having reference to the greatest trade of this country. In language always inflated, and at times bordering on the ridiculous, it points out that during the six years which have elapsed since the Plimsoll legislation, wrecks have increased instead of having diminished, and that the department is unable to cope with them although its expenditure has, by the attempt, been increased to the extent of nearly £60,000 per annum.

It seems that this money has not only been thrown away, but, from the general tone of the notice, may be almost said to have increased the number of wrecks. To rely upon the department is, by its own confession—

BOARD OF TRADE. "To open the floodgates of the Atlantic tide and sweep them out with Mrs. Partington's mop."

And this statement gives a very fair idea of the species of hyperbole with which the notice is literally crammed. It proceeds to state that—

BOARD OF TRADE. "The report of the Wreck Commissioners points to a state of things which the public conscience will not permit to continue."

Now, however powerful the public conscience may be, until it can quell the storms and control the convulsions of nature to which our planet has lately been subjected, it is difficult to see how the withholding of its permission to sink will have the effect of keeping ships afloat.

Then, there is the suggestion that it would be well if the State were to interfere and make bargains between shippers and shipowners, and in reference to this subject the notice says—

BOARD OF TRADE. "If freedom is invoked, as it no doubt would be were any interference with these contracts attempted, the legislature has not hesitated to interfere with similar contracts by Railway Companies."

The department is unable to see the very obvious distinction between the two cases, viz. that in the former one the trader has either to close his works, or submit to any charges the Railway Companies choose to make; whilst in the latter, he enjoys the benefit derived from the unlimited competition of all the ships on the sea.

The claptrap of the day is so wonderfully illustrated by remarks made in further reference to this subject that I reproduce them for the benefit of my readers, viz. :—

> "As to freedom of contract—that most respectable but much-abused phrase—we may ask, in the first place, how much real freedom there is in many of these contracts. When, in the hurry and competition of modern business, a merchant gets a bill of lading, when a passenger takes a ticket, when an underwriter takes a line on a policy, does he, can he, deliberate upon all the terms of his bargain? Does not custom sit upon him with a weight heavy as frost, and deep almost as life—custom which he cannot break through without an effort and a sacrifice which would throw him out in the race?" — BOARD OF TRADE.

Surely no stronger argument for the maintenance of freedom of contract can be adduced than these words, showing, as they do, the hands our business arrangements would fall into were it dispensed with, and England left to compete against the rest of the world with her trade regulated by the paid philosophy of the Board of Trade.

I must ask my readers to compare the above-mentioned sentimental and wholly imaginary evils with the very real and crushing ones comprised in railway monopoly, and to mark how the same hand has dealt with the different sides of the question. If Sir Thomas Farrer possessed a little more knowledge of the world and of practical business, and were a little less imbued with the Governmental notion that the British trader would be benefited by the assistance of his grandmother, he would know that the trading community understands all about "custom" and all about "contracts," and that people who cannot keep in the race without his assistance in explaining these matters to them will most infallibly be left behind.

The general purport of the notice seems to be, that all shipwrecks are preventible, and that they only occur in consequence of the wicked shipowners ensuring ships so that they may gain by their being lost, whilst the insurance companies gain by paying for the loss; and it proceeds to explain this apparent anomaly by saying—

> "It is the greatest mistake to suppose that underwriters as a body have an interest in preventing shipwrecks. So long as premiums bear a fair proportion to risks, the more the losses the more the business of the insurance. If there were no shipwrecks, there would be no underwriting. But the underwriter has a special interest in over-insurance."
>
> BOARD OF TRADE.

This seems to point to the fact that all parties gain by the gigantic loss, except the people who are drowned. The captains and sailors, apparently, lend themselves to the nefarious system in the most accommodating manner, meekly going out to be drowned in the interests of their employers!

Perhaps the transparency of the following extract exemplifies as strongly as any the exaggerative and sensational character of the whole statement. It says—

> "Taking all the sea casualties together, it would probably be no exaggeration to put the money loss to the nation at much more than ten millions a year. Have inferior ship-owners any right to throw away this amount of national property, even if we put the much more serious question of loss of life out of the question?"
>
> BOARD OF TRADE.

This statement brings to light the following curious facts:—

1st. That uninsured ships never go down!

2nd. That, as superior shipowners never lose ships, the money they are in the habit of paying for insurance premiums is parted with for no intelligible reason.

3rd. That, as "inferior shipowners" destroy all the ships which are lost for the purpose of receiving more than their value from Insurance Companies, it follows that if they were unable to insure, they would cease to "throw away" these vessels; *ergo* the Insurance Companies cause all the wrecks which occur upon the ocean.

Having sufficiently alarmed us by these frightful discoveries, Sir Thomas proceeds to administer comfort by hinting that Mr. Chamberlain is prepared with a Bill! The whole thing is very simple! All that is requisite is to deal with these "inferior shipowners," and shipwrecks will become a thing of the past. There will be no more drowned sailors, and the country will be enriched by ten millions a year. He does not inform us whether the Bill will prevent lighthouses being blown down, piers destroyed, houses unroofed, or whether it may have a tendency to prevent another Java catastrophe; but if these matters have been overlooked, possibly a clause might be inserted dealing with them, for there is apparently no evil on the face of the earth for which the Radical does not possess a panacea, if you only let him make an Act of Parliament. In any case, according to Sir Thomas, it is clear that in shipping matters it is the Radicals to whom we must look for help, as the measure proposed by the Conservatives in 1876 would have left the law in an unsatisfactory state; and, besides this, the party were more interested in the Imperial Titles Bill than in saving the lives of our sailors and ten millions a year. This intimation is thus conveyed—

> "But the question must be grasped by no timid hand. An attempt was made in 1876 to deal with this question, but by a measure which, if it had passed, would have left the law in an unsatisfactory state. The Imperial Titles Bill intervened, and the Maritime Contracts Bill dropped. Let us trust that when the subject is taken up again, it will be by stronger hands, and in a more thorough-going and more resolute spirit."

<small>BOARD OF TRADE.</small>

After this, one really begins to wonder what are the duties of a Permanent Secretary.

Apparently, the gentleman who occupies this position at the Board of Trade considers himself a kind of legislative adviser to both Houses of

Parliament and the country generally, and that he can impart to his individual opinion the official weight of the important department in which he happens to be a servant; that it is within his province to advertise the excellencies of the particular Government in power, and at the same time to point to the deficiencies of its predecessors.

It is, however, high time that this pert officialism is stopped.

If monopolies are to be protected, and freetraders harassed, there are always plenty of people in Parliament ready to assist in the operation, but it is unbearable that Governmental departments should be converted into weapons of defence or attack. It is, of course, only natural that Sir Thomas should be duly grateful to the Government for his baronetcy, but this by no means justifies him in publicly taking up the cudgels, either for the Liberals, against the Conservatives, or for one portion of the community against another, as he is equally the servant of all.

Now, with regard to the proposed legislation, it cannot be denied that there have been cases of overloading, and over-insuring, so that the loss of a vessel has resulted in gain to the owner. There have also been cases of arson in which the loss of a house has resulted in gain to the householder. Crime always has existed, and, I fear, always will more or less exist, in every grade of society, but proof that it sometimes takes the form of overloading no more justifies the sweeping charges brought against the shipowners, than evidence that it sometimes takes the form of arson would justify similar charges against the householders.

It is perfectly ridiculous to suppose, that notwithstanding an extra £60,000 a year is spent by the Board of Trade for the detection and prevention of this particular species of maritime crime, captains and sailors would stand quietly by whilst it is being deliberately planned that they should watch preparations being made for their own destruction, and yet never call the attention of the authorities to the matter.

Interference with insurance, which is apparently part of the proposed legislation, would simply mean taking away a considerable portion of the shipping trade from Great Britain and handing it over to the foreigner; and, if insurance is only a synonym for drowning, there would be nothing to prevent his employing British sailors, and continuing both processes on the elaborate system of the British shipowner as described in the departmental notice of the Board of Trade.

THE EDUCATION ACT OF 1870.

THE passing of this Act involved to the general community, and especially to capitalists and working men, consequences little thought of at the time, and which are even now only partially understood. The measure and its subsequent amendments being carried during periods of excitement and fictitious prosperity, the public mind was peculiarly unfitted for calm and judicial inquiry, and for a due appreciation of the gravity of their ultimate effects upon the country.

In consequence (probably, of the Franco-Prussian war), the commerce of England had not only increased by "leaps and bounds," but gold was literally beginning to pour into the laps of traders and the working classes generally; and the Radical, ever ready to use the passing and illusory circumstances of the moment as a basis for legislation, managed to persuade the people of England that they could not only easily afford to lose the products of children's labour, but could as easily pay, in additional taxes, the sum required for educational purposes.

The direct consequences of the measure were in themselves serious enough, but, by the appointment of an educational enthusiast as Minister of Education, the present Government have added point to its defects to an extent which has resulted not only in the Act becoming a crushing burden to the country, but in its being used, doubtless with the best intentions, as an engine of injury and cruelty to thousands of helpless children. The newspapers have recently literally teemed with letters, of which the following one, addressed to the *School Guardian*, may be taken as a fair sample. It is headed " Board School, Pesnett, Dudley," and is as follows :—

" SIR,

"Will you kindly find room for the following painful narrative ? In passing through the Standard I. room yesterday morning during the recess, about eleven o'clock, I observed a little girl crying and evidently very unwell, in a corner of the room. Without delay, I sent her home in charge of another girl, cancelling her attendance. In coming to school this morning, a little after eight I was informed to my horror that she died about five o'clock. After twelve, I went direct to the house, and was informed by her sorrowing parents of the nature and symptoms of her illness. During the time, she talked and raved over her school work, uttering occasionally, almost with her last breath, 'I can't do it; I can't do it!' I then went to her medical attendant, a gentleman highly respected in this neighbourhood, who has kindly furnished me with the following certificate :—

"' *The Poplars, Pesnett.*

"'This is to certify that I was called in on November 8, 1883, to attend Sophia Raybould, aged six and a half years, who died this morning, after nineteen hours' suffering from acute meningitis and convulsions. My opinion is, that the present system of cramming children under the Education Act now in existence is very injurious to the brains of children of such tender years. I have had similar cases to the above previously.

"'(*Signed*)   J. BRADLEY, Surgeon.'

"I may add that this is my second victim.

What sufferings and misery may have been undergone by others to whom death may not have brought relief, none can tell.

"Mr. Mundella may discredit, statesmen may ignore, inspectors after twenty years' experience may deny the existence of a single case of high pressure; but facts are against them. How can they know from an annual visit to a school? They guess and grope; we see and know. This fresh appeal to their attention and sympathy will probably pass, as hundreds of like cases have passed before. But of this I am sure, that unless our appeal is listened to, and at no distant date, a Higher than man will, by some rude awakening which we little anticipate, step in and save us from the scenes of torture and misery of which we are daily the unwilling witnesses.

"(*Signed*) DAVID CLARK."

Even Mr. Matthew Arnold, one of our best known inspectors and a Liberal of Liberals, thus writes: "Bodily exercise and recreation deserve far more care in our schools than they receive. We take too little thought for the bodies of our school children; we are too intent on forcing more and still more into their minds, unregardful how easily the attention at their age may be overtired."

Teachers have, however, no option in the matter. On they must go or lose their salary, and in order to keep their place in what has been described as a "literal death struggle," they are compelled to resort to the practice of giving children lessons to prepare at home. My readers can imagine the bitter misery which this system may entail upon these half-starved little creatures, struggling in their wretchedly lit and squalid homes to prepare their tasks on pain of being flogged next day. Mr. Mundella was recently interrogated on the question in the House of Commons, and is reported by the newspapers to have said—

"Where school managers have required that reasonable home lessons shall be learnt by children in a good state of health, the Education Department has always supported them in maintaining their rules and preserving the discipline of their schools."

MR. LEIGHTON. "Against the will of the parents? Are these lessons insisted on against the will of the parents?"

MR. MUNDELLA. "If the parent is not satisfied

with that school, he can send his child to some other." (Loud cries of "Oh!") "We do not find that parents object. It is other people who object, not the parents." (Much dissent.)

Now, who is to decide whether the home lessons are "reasonable," or the children in a "good state of health"? or what power have the teachers of knowing whether the parents even provide the light of an ordinary dip candle in the preparation of their lessons? Referring to this matter subsequently in a speech at Peterborough, Mr. Mundella, with true Radical unction, justified the system by saying "It was our duty to see that our children were not worse equipped for the battle of life than children of other countries." But here he distinctly misses the point! The contention is, that the "equipment" provided by the Education Department, in too many instances, renders any such preparation for life unnecessary, and that these poor little beings fight their only "battle of life" with the schoolmaster, and, like Sophia Raybould, often perish in the conflict.

Mr. Mundella's new code, which is calling forth protests from all parts of the country, is described by a very competent authority engaged in carrying out its provisions in the following words:—

"The code is framed as if all children were alike in capacity. It is a painful thing to see the work too hard for a boy, and yet, as a penalty for passing the last standard, on he must go at the next, although his teacher is certain he is mentally unfit for it."

The Committee of the Union of Elementary Teachers, in formally protesting against it to the lords of the Education Department, point out that its requirements are excessive, and lead to undue pressure upon the children, placing heavy burdens on such among them as are weak of body and slow of brain. One would have naturally supposed that a report of this kind, from a body so eminently qualified to understand the practical working of the code, and substantiated by independent testimony from all parts of England, would have had due weight with "my lords"; but their lordships' reply is not in accordance with this idea, reminding one rather of the answer of an irate schoolmistress than a department of state, and in words strongly suggestive of copy-book morality, the council was told that "zealous teachers make good scholars," and that it was the business of the former to inspire the whole of the surrounding country neighbourhood with an enthusiastic love of learning, both in school and out of school, and that the teachers were at fault—not the system!

Having demolished the teachers by this characteristic specimen of Radical cant, Mr. Mundella, with the object apparently of distracting public attention from the subject, proceeded to stump the country and deliver a series of lectures of the "mothers' meeting" type in favour of education. If this gentleman is to be allowed to continue in his wild career, urging his educational craze on and still on, we may expect soon to arrive at the halcyon days to which certain Radical members of Parliament already point, when the annual grant for educational purposes shall equal that of our standing army. On the introduction of the Bill, the cost to the ratepayer was not to exceed a halfpenny in the pound, but in London it is now about eightpence; and a member of the London School Board, in a letter to the *Christian Age*, furnishes a few interesting details. He says, "The solicitor of the Board, in addition to a salary of £1,500 per annum, was entitled to receive four per cent. on all sites on which schools were to be erected, and up to November, 1882, he had actually received, exclusive of counsel's fees, the enormous sum of £101,000. This per centage is now reduced from four to two; but his demand for four per cent. will extend for years to come, as he claims from the time when notice was given to treat for the sites. In the bye-laws department, £32,000 is spent annually in paying 'visitors' to compel parents to send their children to the Board Schools. In the architects' department, the aggregate sum spent in salaries is upwards of £10,000 per annum. As to the training-ship *Shaftesbury*, it was at first decided that the expenditure was not to exceed £7,000; but such has been the gross mismanagement, that bills have been sent in for upwards of £50,000."

Prior to 1870 and the introduction of School Boards, the total expenditure for education purposes in this country was only about a million and a half; while in the present year, the expenditure in London alone will amount to very nearly a million of money! There is, however, no necessity to expatiate on the woful way in which the country was deceived as to the cost of our School Boards, the fact being only too well known and appreciated.

Quite apart, however, from any ratepayers'

question, the Act itself has injured this country to an incalculable extent, and has formed no inconsiderable a factor in bringing about the decadence of our trade and agriculture. Is it to be expected that, having denuded ourselves of the advantages derived from cheap labour, we can compete with foreign countries, as in the days of our prosperity? Is it possible that any country can bear the sudden withdrawal of the annual millions hitherto earned by its children, and go on just as if nothing had happened? By law, no boy is allowed to go to work (except as a half-timer) until he has reached the age of fourteen (or passed an educational standard); and in the experience derived from the practical operation of this law, the people of England have learned that, as usual, there is another side to the pictorial blessings which accompany the introduction of great Radical measures.

No one denies that a certain amount of elementary education (viz. to the extent of what is familiarly known as "the three R's") should be imparted to every child; but to decree that strong and active boys shall be compelled to loaf about the streets and highways until they arrive at the age at which respectable tradesmen's sons, in the days of England's prosperity, were accustomed to leave school, is not only to strike a cruel blow at the welfare of the country, but tends directly to the injury of the boys themselves. Neither traders nor farmers can obtain a sufficiency of boy labour, and men have to be paid for doing boys' work. In the coal and iron districts, the effects are disastrous in the extreme, and the scarcity of boys, for work in which it is almost impossible for men to supply their place, leads to the greatest difficulties. It is now quite a common thing for pony drivers and trappers to stop important collieries, and the industries depending on them (thus throwing hundreds of people out of work), simply because the lads are conscious that, owing to the artificial scarcity of their labour, they can practically dictate their own terms. The following report of a conviction, for employing boys under age, will give some idea of the difficulties which beset agriculture:—

"Mr. Charles Walker, a large farmer, of Lound, near Retford, was fined one pound on Saturday for employing two boys, named Whitehead, aged ten, and Taylor, twelve. Defendant said it was impossible for agriculturists to farm, if they could not employ village lads at certain times. It was only the other day that the clerk to the Thorne Board of Guardians said if the Act were carried out, he would have to summon the whole parish. Colonel Eyre remarked that the magistrates were there for the purpose of administering the law. Mr. Walker—'A liberal law and a most absurd law.'"

At the present time, the produce of our general industries are sold at prices lower than were ever known within memory, whilst the wages paid to our workpeople are far higher than they were a few years ago. It follows, therefore, that the position of capitalists is the reverse of satisfactory—innumerable failures, the closing of works, and the blowing out of blast furnaces, etc., testifying only too surely to the fact.

On the other hand, our workpeople, who could live in comparative ease and comfort on the lower wages of former times, are now unable to do so on higher ones, and are constantly either striking for wages which capitalists are unable to pay, or emigrating to foreign counties; and the reason for all this is not far to seek. A working man's family formerly meant wealth to himself and his employer, but it now means a burden and an expense to both.

A colliery manager of large experience recently said to me, " These boys of fourteen are no use to me now. They have certainly learnt something, and that is, how to do nothing ; and before one has time to teach them their work, they consider themselves men, and require men's wages."

If there is no mystic significance attaching to the number fourteen, the age alluded to must be presumed to have been fixed because of its reasonableness. Now, comparing the present commercial and agricultural position of the country with that of the period in which the Education Act and its subsequent amendments were passed, does it not follow that an age which was reasonable then is wholly unreasonable now ? If the question of reasonableness, however, does not enter into the calculation, and the greater the age the nearer the educational elysium, why not make it twenty-one at once ? It must be remembered that boys who have not been able to pass the fourth standard before arriving at the age of fourteen, must either be idle or dull of comprehension, and although probably admirably adapted for manual labour, are not of the sort from which scholars are made, and by enforced idleness are simply unfitted for the work which Nature intended them to perform.

The Education Department, however, seems to be of the opinion that unless all our future "hewers of wood and drawers of water" are crammed with useless accomplishments and put through the regulation amount of poetry, philosophy, mathematics, etc., etc., possibly some genius, hidden in their teeming thousands, may miss making his mark in the world. There need, however, be no great anxiety on this account. George Stephenson, Dr. Whewell, late Master of Trinity, and thousands of lesser lights, all prove that genius can come to the front without the assistance of Mr. Mundella.

Not only did an immense proportion of the managers of our largest works and industries commence labour at an extremely early age, and without any educational forcing, but also a considerable number of our members of Parliament.

But even supposing some stray genius here and there among the masses is so peculiarly constituted as to be unable to force his way unless crammed by the Board School until he is fourteen, what is the loss involved compared to the evils I have alluded to? Will the advantages derived by society from the brain of this tardily developed genius compensate for the half-starving of hundreds of duller boys and their widowed mothers? will it recompense the country for the enormous loss caused to its trade and agriculture? For the moment the country is certainly not suffering from lack of genius. We have enough and to spare in the House of Commons, besides being absolutely surfeited with it in the Government. What we lack and lack badly is common sense, and this, I am afraid, neither Mr. Mundella nor his patent process are likely to provide for us.

It is high time, and indeed the present state of the country renders it absolutely necessary, that an alteration should be made in the age at which boys may commence to earn their bread; it is equally necessary on the score of humanity that the merciless provisions of Mr. Mundella's code should be relaxed; and these are questions upon which candidates at the next election will be probably asked to express a very definite opinion.

MR. CHAMBERLAIN'S PROPOSED RAILWAY LEGISLATION.

In connection with this subject, the following letter from Mr. Chamberlain (to a gentleman in Birmingham) has appeared in the *Times*:—

MR. CHAM-BERLAIN.
"I am in receipt of your favour of the 8th inst., with enclosed copy of your letter, which I had already seen in the *Daily Post*. I am aware of the numerous complaints of preferential rates, but, of course, am not in a position to give any opinion in any particular case as to which I have no sufficient information. I do not quite understand why a case is not taken before the Railway Commissioners, who are authorized to deal with unfair preferences. The whole subject of railway legislation will come before Parliament next session, as I propose to introduce a Bill to extend the powers of Railway Commissioners and for other purposes. It is evident there will be much opposition, and unless I am cordially supported by the trade and the country, I cannot hope to carry my proposals."

Now, if, during the considerable period which has elapsed since the appointment of the Select

Committee on Railway Rates and Fares in 1881, Mr. Chamberlain had devoted rather less time to the philosophical consideration of the doctrine of "unearned increment" and other similar theories, he would probably have had sufficient leisure to gather from the exhaustive evidence of British and Irish traders the reason why cases are not brought before the Railway Commission, and the paragraph in the *Pall Mall Gazette* (a paper generally regarded as the especial mouthpiece of Mr. Chamberlain) in reference to the aforesaid letter might have been unnecessary. It is as follows :—

<blockquote>
"The President of the Board of Trade appeals very frankly to the trade of the country to back him up in the legislation which he promises to introduce next session, for the extension of the powers of the Railway Commission and for other purposes. To this measure he says he foresees that there will be much opposition, and he can do nothing unless he is energetically supported. Chambers of commerce, trade associations, and the public generally, will do well to take note of Mr. Chamberlain's appeal, and support him as energetically as possible against the machinations of Sir Edward Watkin and his directors and associations." — PALL MALL GAZETTE.
</blockquote>

Mr. Chamberlain, as usual, appears to be unable to approach the consideration of any great public question without, in the first place, making use of it as a means of personal attack, and the passage of arms which recently occurred between Sir Edward Watkin and himself probably accounts for the former gentleman being held up to public notice as the incarnation of all that is wrong in our railway system. Evil and injurious as the action of individuals or particular companies may be, and often is, in its effect on trade in certain localities, the issue now before the public embraces the far more serious question involved in our system of railway government, which renders such action possible, and gives the carrying trade a direct and despotic control over all the other trades in the country, and compared to which individual "machinations" are of small moment. However, this letter and newspaper paragraph shows a decided change of front, since Sir Thomas Farrer indulged in his elaborate defence of the preferential system with the tacit consent of Mr. Chamberlain and the warm approval of the *Pall Mall Gazette*.

The explanation of the altered attitude may possibly be found in the following fact, viz. that at the time Sir Thomas Farrer's views were made public, the whole of the information received by the Select Committee was buried in a few stray blue books (the evidence being out of print within a very few days of the time in which the committee's report appeared), and Sir Thomas had thus practically the whole field to himself.

Since, however, these pages were commenced, several gentlemen on intimate terms with Mr. Chamberlain were cognisant that the portions of the evidence given in them were being reproduced, for the inspection and consideration of the public; and it is possible that this fact coming to Mr. Chamberlain's ears may have caused him to think it prudent to evince some slight interest in the matter. However this may be, the important question is, What does he now propose to do? He speaks of "a Bill for extending the powers of the Railway Commissioners" and for "other purposes;" but *unless* the bill provides for equality in railway charges, *unless* it decrees that no Railway Company shall charge for similar services a higher rate to one person than to another, and *unless* it brings it within the power of all to obtain justice and compel the companies to obey the law, the new Act will become equally as useless as those which preceded it.

The issue between the public and the Railway Companies, although very narrow and intelligible, is for some reason or other apparently quite beyond the grasp of our legislators, whose assistance is invariably confined to offers of relief for anywhere except the particular place in which the shoe pinches. The proposed Bill promises in this respect to differ in no way from its predecessors. A deputation from the Railway Companies having already promised Mr. Chamberlain to appoint a committee to assist him in its preparation, and thus (with the additional superintendence of Sir Thomas Farrer) to provide sufficient guarantee for the retention of all the ancient landmarks.

This, however, is not a species of preparation likely to commend the Bill to the acceptance of the public; and however successful similar tactics may have been in the past, the existing state of trade renders it highly improbable that in the future the country will consent to be duped in so barefaced and ridiculous a manner.

The subject being of such vital importance, and surrounded as it is by the cloud of mysteries designedly prepared by the Railway Companies for their own protection, I will now, even at the risk of repetition, proceed to state, in as few words as possible, the real issue between the public and themselves.

I will admit that the country possesses a Railway Court and sufficient Acts of Parliament in relation to equality, maximum charges, terminal charges, etc., etc. It is a fact, nevertheless, that Railway Companies have hitherto successfully withstood the restraining influence of all these institutions; and the question which now presents itself is, Supposing that they continue in the future to exhibit the same indifference to the law that they have shown in the past, are they to be permitted to enjoy similar impunity? Are they to exercise uncontrolled powers of charging until some particular individual chooses to prosecute them and incur, before the Railway Commissioners, the enormous costs involved in determining the exact definition of the word "reasonable;" and are they (even after the successful operation of an isolated prosecution of the kind) to be allowed still to exercise despotic sway over all traders who cannot afford similar costs?

If these questions are to be answered in the negative, then there must be no ambiguity in railway charges. The companies must be compelled to publish a list of all their charges applicable to every trader on their system, and equal to all for the carriage of similar goods over similar distances.

There is no middle course, and the slightest variation or the introduction of the smallest element of uncertainty at once removes the question of illegality from the jurisdiction of the local courts (the only one within the reach of ninety-nine traders out of every hundred), and transfers them to the Railway Commission, a tribunal which the Railway Companies have already managed to endow with all the terrors appertaining to costs and to uncertainty.

This is the direct issue which the country has to determine, and any extension of the power of the Railway Commission (although most useful for deciding matters of principle, ambiguities in Acts of Parliament, or the general question of reasonableness in which large bodies of traders are simultaneously interested, and which collectively they are perfectly able to bring before the commissioners) will not have the slightest effect in compelling Railway Companies to keep within the law in their action towards individuals.

I can give no better illustration of the truth of my contention than by referring to the position of boatmen, who conduct their business on canals belonging to the Railway Companies. In these cases, the latter merely act as toll-takers, and are only authorized by their Acts to charge for the use of the water at the rate of so much per ton per mile, undue preference being prohibited under heavy penalties.

Here, therefore, there is no question of terminal charges or comparative expenses between long and short distances, and yet the companies do not for an instant scruple to charge far higher mileage rates on one portion of a canal than on another, regulating their charges either for the purpose of crushing competition at some particular point, favouring certain individuals, or in any other way suiting their own convenience.

Is it reasonable to suppose that these poor boatmen, whose whole capital probably consists in a certain share of the barges they employ, can afford to incur the expense of taking questions of the kind before the Railway Commission?

On the other hand, it is abundantly plain that a published list of mileage charges, equal to all over the whole length of the navigation, would give these men a simple and easy remedy in case of any infraction of the law by the companies.

On the subject of canals, I must ask my readers to carefully consider the exhaustive evidence of Mr. Spence, commencing on p. 112, and his proposal that the Government should purchase the canals from the Railway Companies, and by deepening them where necessary (for the purpose of admitting ocean-going steamers) produce a system of cheap and competitive carriage, which would go far to revolutionize the whole trade of the kingdom. Nations which compete with England have the full advantage of this cheapest of all means of traffic; and the sanction given by Parliament to Railway Companies for its practical suppression here, is probably as strong an instance as can be adduced of the extraordinary apathy evinced by our legislators in regard to the trading interests of this country. The adoption of Mr. Spence's proposal would not only exercise a most salutary effect upon our trade, but would be the means of providing employment for the many thousands of labouring men who are now unable to find work.

In Ireland it would go far to solve the difficulties of the present situation, in providing a cheap means of access to the markets for the farmer, work for the labourer, and profitable investment for the Government.

Important, however, as this and the various kindred questions are, it is not to be conceived for a moment that they will be dealt with satisfactorily by the present Parliament, and the whole tone of Mr. Chamberlain's letter and conduct shows clearly that the question is not one likely to be included in the Radical shibboleth. Anxious as that gentleman is to pose before the country as an ardent and drastic reformer, he does not apparently regard these matters as congenial subjects for extra parliamentary speeches, philippics in the *Fortnightly Review*, or fulminatory notices from the Board of Trade.

If in Ireland the Government had compelled the Railway Companies to obey the law, the people would have benefited pecuniarily to an enormously greater extent than by the reductions in rent awarded by the Land Commissioners, and the advantages would not only have been common to both present and future tenants, but the whole nation would have participated in the general impetus given to both trade and agriculture. This was, of course, thoroughly understood at the time; but after doing a sum in simple addition (viz. by adding the number of Railway Directors in the House of Commons to the number of their Parliamentary supporters), the Government arrived at the conclusion that the safer plan would be to confiscate the money of the landlords and allow the Railway Companies to remain as they were.

Mr. Chamberlain, for the same reason, doubtless recognizes that it is safer to expend his reforming zeal in attacks on traders, or property in general, rather than expose the Government to the dangers they must necessarily incur in protecting this country from the species of extortion to which it is now subjected.

Cheapness of transit is unquestionably one of the most important elements necessary to the commercial success of a country, and it is equally obvious that Great Britain suffers more severely from the absence of this essential factor than any other civilized country in the world. So long, however, as the constituencies persist in garrisoning St. Stephens with men who (irrespective of politics) are determined to uphold their own monopolies against the interest of the public at large, so long will the trade of the country continue to decline.

CONCLUDING REMARKS.

IN bringing these remarks to a conclusion, I would respectfully urge upon my readers, in view of the all-important issues to which I have alluded, that in no single instance should the opportunity be lost of *making them test questions at the next election.* Above all, the effects on this country involved in the system of railway autocracy allied with (one-sided) free trade should be fully considered, and upon that unholy alliance the electors should pronounce judgment clearly and definitely, without allowing themselves to be lulled into a false sense of security, or permitting their opinions to be affected in the slightest degree by the apparent apathy of Parliament.

The facts relating to the manufacture of English necessaries from English material in foreign countries are proofs strong as Holy Writ of an inherent and radical fallacy in our commercial system, but notorious and ever-increasing as are these facts and proofs, they have hitherto failed to create the slightest effect upon the mind of Parliament; and my readers may rest assured that while the Legislature continues to be composed so largely of monopolists, the eyes of Parliament will remain resolutely closed until the ruin of the country eventuates in the ruin of the monopolies.

It is, therefore, of paramount importance that upon this question the electors should think for themselves, and not sit with folded hands waiting for a sign from Government, for that sign will never be given.

The question is one entirely in the hands of the constituencies. They can either elect members with sole reference to their opinions in regard to any particular specimen of legislative quackery on which the country may be appealed to, or on the other hand, they may return representatives who will inform the Government, in plain and unmistakable terms, that the country is wearied with measures introduced by Radical wire-pullers for the sole purpose of providing excitement for the Caucuses, to the complete exclusion of all questions relating to its trading and commercial interests. The English people expect and insist that in laws affecting commerce they shall be placed on a par with other commercial nations; and that even if the advantages derived from the possession of the richest mineral fields in the world are insufficient to enable them to manufacture, as in former days, for the greater portion of the civilized globe, they shall at least enjoy the modest privileges included in the right to manufacture their own iron with their own coal, and to use their own railways on equal terms with their foreign competitors.

The key-note to some of these questions has already been struck in the very home of the Caucus—not, however, by the once traders (now pseudo-philosophers) who represent the town of Birmingham, but the duty of giving prominence to commercial questions in that industrial centre has fallen to the duty of a Conservative nobleman. It is to be hoped that his warning words and the plain unvarnished stories of the traders and farmers, to which I have alluded, and which form but a faint reflex of the "bitter cry" arising from all parts of the country, may have some influence in arresting the decay of British commerce; and that the united action of the constituencies will prevent the natural resources of this country from being treated as so much raw material dedicated to the express use of foreign nations, and England itself from being turned into a mere receptacle for the goods into which that material is manufactured.

THE END.

www.ingramcontent.com/pod-product-compliance
Lightning Source LLC
Chambersburg PA
CBHW020310240426
43673CB00039B/766